Amy LaBelle has the magic touch when it comes to weddings—and now you can, too.

—**Christine Lusita,** Lifestyle Contributor, *Access Daily, California Live, Us Weekly*

I savor good wine and delight in witnessing an elegant wedding. Amy LaBelle has combined these two miraculous things to create this elegant book, which you will savor.

—**David M. Corbin,** #1 *Wall Street Journal* bestselling author and mentor to mentors

Dear Reader,

Congratulations on your engagement, and best wishes to you as you plan your wedding day! I wrote this book to be a guide for you as you begin to make decisions and plans for your celebration. My sincere hope is that you find inspiration in these pages that help you choose a wine theme for your wedding.

As a winemaker, wedding venue owner, and planner, I have seen it all, and I hope my advice in the pages that follow feels as if you are talking to a very experienced big sister—one who can help! I'm excited for us to dive in and begin dreaming about your special day, a day filled with many touches that help you manifest the celebration of which you have always dreamed.

Let's get started!

Amy

WINE WEDDINGS

THE ULTIMATE GUIDE TO
CREATING THE WINE-THEMED WEDDING OF YOUR DREAMS

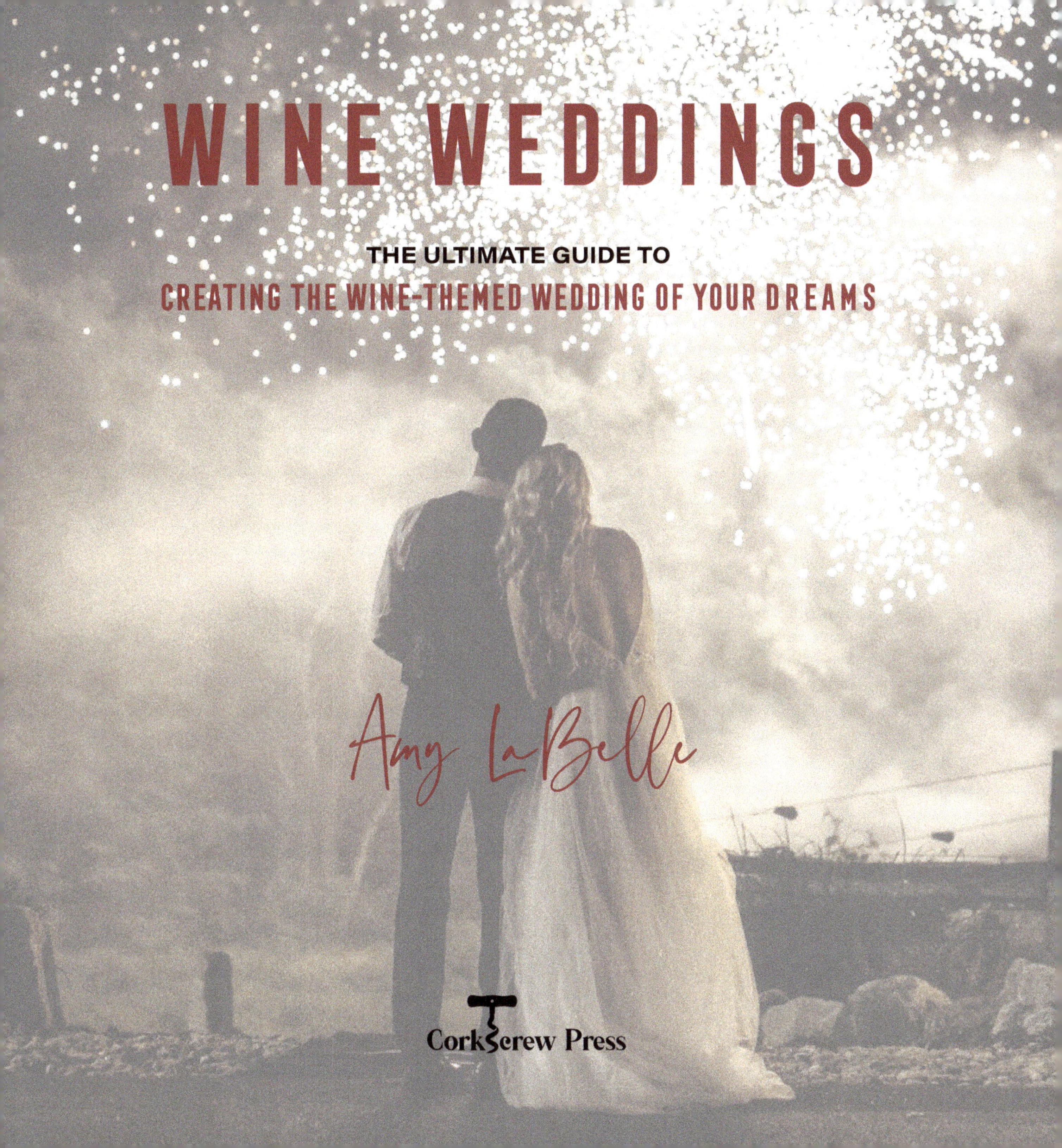

Amy LaBelle

CorkScrew Press

Copyright ©2023 by Amy LaBelle

All rights reserved. No part of this book may be used or reproduced in any manner whatsoever without written permission except in the case of brief quotations embodied in critical articles or reviews.

Published by Corkscrew Press.

Produced by GMK Writing and Editing, Inc.
Managing Editor: Katie Benoit
Edited by: Holly Rubino
Copyedited by Cindi Pietrzyk
Proofread by Amy Paradysz
Text design and composition by Libby Kingsbury
Cover design by Libby Kingsbury
Printed by IngramSpark

Print ISBN: 979-8-9861737-9-5
Ebook EISN: 979-8-9863472-0-2

Visit labellewinery.com and amylabelle.com for information.
Write the author at amy@labellewinery.com or 14 Route 111, Derry, NH 03080

Note: *This publication is presented solely for informational, educational, and entertainment purposes. It is not intended to provide personal, relationship, legal, financial, or other advice and should not be relied upon as such. If expert assistance is required, the services of a professional should be sought. The publisher and the author and their affiliated entities and individuals do not make any guarantees or other promises as to any results that may be obtained from using the content or recommendations of this book. To the maximum extent permitted by law, the publisher and the author and their affiliated entities and individuals disclaim any and all liability in the event any information contained in this book proves to be inaccurate, incomplete, or unreliable, or results in any harm or loss. You, the reader, are responsible for your own choices, actions, and results.*

"All my life I thought that the story was over when the hero and heroine were safely engaged—after all, what's good enough for Jane Austen ought to be good enough for anyone. But it's a lie. The story is about to begin, and every day will be a new piece of the plot."

—Mary Ann Shaffer, *The Guernsey Literary and Potato Peel Pie Society*

"A good marriage does not happen spontaneously. It is crafted and created every single day with love and effort. Though you will be very busy planning your wedding for the next many months, don't forget to tend your relationship and plan for your marriage, too! Your wedding is one day; your marriage is forever."

—Amy LaBelle

Heather Donald Photography

To my Cesar Alejandro, who has shown me that true, authentic love is a real thing and who is the best partner in every possible way. I still love making coffee for you every morning.

And to my boys, Jackson Alejandro and Lucas Cesar, I hope I make you proud.

ACKNOWLEDGMENTS

Writing a book is a massive undertaking and often feels like a lonely journey. But this has not been so in this case. Many people have helped me along the way.

Thank you to Gary M. Krebs for believing in my idea and putting me on the right path. Thank you, Amy Prenner and Jess Ponce for ensuring that the world knows about this book. Thank you to Holly Rubino for your skilled editing. Thank you to Libby Kingsbury for your beautiful design work and helping me create a book I love.

To the LaBelle Winery Team, a million thank-yous for your excellence now and always in executing the most beautiful weddings for our couples. Your dedication inspires me every day!

Thank you to Danielle Sullivan, who worked alongside me to make this book possible and who poured through thousands of photos to help illustrate the wine wedding concept. I love working with you, Danielle! Thanks for always making my big ideas happen, from this book to LaBelle Lights, and for taking on national publicity.

Thank you to James Mojonnier, who provided the beautiful graphics, some photos, and photo editing for this book. Your artistry and eye constantly impress me, and I am grateful to have you on my team and to count you as a friend.

Thank you to Michelle Thornton for standing behind my big dreams as my brand director for the past decade. Your steady hand and measured approach balance my wild imaginings so well. Your dedication to growing the LaBelle brand is impressive and appreciated, and your friendship is a very important part of my life.

◀ *Love, Annaliese Photography*

Thank you to Kim Cortino, who built the LaBelle Winery Wedding program alongside me, and who, herself, was a LaBelle bride (you will see some of her wedding photos in these pages). Thank you for your stellar dedication to excellence and for letting me use your photos. Your wedding brought us together as friends, and I love watching your career and your loving family grow.

Thank *you* for reading my book and for incorporating a wine theme into your beautiful wedding plans. I wish you the very best day ever and will be toasting you in spirit.

Finally, to my family, Cesar Arboleda and my two boys, Jackson and Lucas, my endless love and gratitude for your enthusiasm and support for my work. I do it all for you.

John Murzaku

CONTENTS

INTRODUCTION:	Getting Excited for Your *Big Day!*, 1
CHAPTER ONE:	Choosing a Wine Theme—Why Theme Your Wedding?, 5
CHAPTER TWO:	Creating a Wine Wedding Theme and Color Scheme, 13
CHAPTER THREE:	Selecting a Venue and Ceremony Site, 29
CHAPTER FOUR:	Dressing the Bridal Party and Welcoming Traveling Guests, 39
CHAPTER FIVE:	Creating Unique Wine-Themed Décor, 47
CHAPTER SIX:	Planning a Meaningful Wine-Themed Rehearsal Dinner, 57
CHAPTER SEVEN:	Setting the Mood with a Vineyard or Winery Ceremony, 67
CHAPTER EIGHT:	Enjoying a Spectacular Cocktail Hour, 77
CHAPTER NINE:	Celebrating in (Wine) Style, 105
CHAPTER TEN:	Designing Wine-Themed Thank-You Notes, 125
	Conclusion, 133
	Wine-Themed Wedding Checklist, 135
	About the Author, 137
	About LaBelle Winery, 139

Dachowski Photography

INTRODUCTION

Getting Excited for Your Big Day!

Congratulations on your engagement! If you are reading this book, you must be getting ready for an incredibly special wedding day! Or perhaps you are assisting someone with planning the wedding. I would like to assist you along this journey with a few tips and tricks I've learned throughout many years working in the wedding industry. I will help you make choices that will keep your wine-themed wedding design process stress-free. Together, you and I can create the wine wedding of your dreams.

I have always loved to dream up parties and events. I become giddy with excitement thinking about the details, from selecting the food, wine, and décor, to creating guest lists and setting the mood. When I was a child, I loved to help prepare appetizers for parties my parents hosted and then serve them on platters as I mingled with adult guests. I carried the love of entertaining into my young adulthood, hosting everything from cocktail parties to Oscars-watching parties, to multiple-floor apartment parties with my neighbors in my Boston brownstone condo (I lived on the "dessert" floor).

Now, I am the founder of and winemaker at LaBelle Winery. How did I get into the wine business? My journey began in 2001 when, on a summer's trip to Nova Scotia, Canada, my dream to become a winemaker was born. I was practicing law in Boston, at the time and was enjoying my vacation. One day I happened upon a tiny winery down a dirt road on my way to Halifax in my little red convertible, which I had driven onto the ferry to Nova Scotia. When I walked into that small winery, no more than 1,100 square feet, the sights, the aromas, the people, and the delicious wine all came together like a lightning bolt over my head. The skies parted, the angels appeared, and I knew in that moment what I wanted to do with my life: I wanted to be a winemaker. But, even more, I wanted to create a hospitality destination that centered around excellent wine and food. A place where community would gather, friends would meet, and families would celebrate. A place to learn, grow, and build community.

It took 4,083 days from that moment in Nova Scotia to the opening of my dream winery in Amherst, New Hampshire, in 2012. Why do I know the number of days? I counted them because I forced myself to do at least one thing every single day to bring my big dream to life.

I didn't stop there, though. I wanted more, so I set my sites on opening another winery, this time in Derry, New Hampshire. During it all, I was able to fulfill my dreams of entertaining. Between the opening of LaBelle Winery in Amherst and the opening of our winery in Derry in 2021, I planned and hosted over a thousand weddings and more than three thousand events in total.

I especially loved planning my wedding to my beloved husband, Cesar Arboleda. We wed on September 2, 2006, and building from that experience I have assembled an events team that is the best in New England. At LaBelle Winery, we take weddings very seriously, catering to every single detail to make your wedding unique and exactly as you wish it to be. Our goal is simple: to ensure you enjoy every moment of one of the most important days of your life!

In the following pages, I'll share with you the secrets to building and planning a perfect, stress-free celebration to kick off your marriage in style. I hope my passion for wine and my love for events planning make the preparation for your wedding a breeze.

Heather Donald Photography

Dachowski Photography

CHAPTER ONE

Choosing a Wine Theme— Why Theme Your Wedding?

Like your unique love, wine is timeless.

A single bottle of wine captures a moment in time that will not be repeated. In it is the very essence of Mother Nature who provided the sun and the rain that caused the grapes to grow, the vineyard workers who picked

Vineyard weddings are perfectly picturesque. *Millyard Studios*

A wine cellar can make an intriguing photo location. *Sam Earp*

the grapes, the winemakers who lost sleep creating their art, and the countless cellar workers and delivery people who eventually brought the bottle to your local wine store or winery's shelves. These workers' stories live on in this beautiful beverage we call wine, and the love of their craft can be tasted in the result of their labors. Winemaking is an art, a labor of love. And its timeless nature can convey a sense of elegance to your wedding day.

As the owner and winemaker at LaBelle Winery, I've seen every style of wedding imaginable over the last decade at my events venue, which sits atop the hillside of our beautiful vineyard. There have been beautiful weddings, elegant weddings, corny weddings, weird weddings, Halloween-themed weddings, holiday weddings, Disney-themed weddings, color-themed weddings, and architecture-themed weddings. You see, not all couples who choose to have a wedding at a winery have a "wine wedding."

AMY'S FAVORITE TOUCHES

Use a wedding planning notebook to store all random thoughts, checklists, and to-do lists from the very beginning, so everything you plan will be in one place. Don't rely on memory!

Some of these weddings have been awesome, beauties to behold, and came together with grace to create a special event that lives on in the memories of those who attended. Others never seemed to gel properly, and guests were left with a not-so-memorable impression. Worse, the couple was left with a sense of regret that their special day would not stand the test of time when they looked at their wedding album years later.

Because I see so many weddings annually and have the privilege of working with so many awesome couples, I also get to see the emotions of the couples on the days leading up to and including the wedding day. Certainly, there is much joy. But often, couples find themselves overwhelmed with the planning details and feel immense pressure. This pressure comes from family expectations, to some degree, and from the thought that since they are spending so much money on one day that everything has to be perfect. Modern couples also face the expectations set by what they see on Pinterest, Instagram, and myriad other websites that set impossibly high standards for weddings. What couples don't know is that many of the photos on these sites are staged by professional stylists or shot in a studio. Some couples

LaBelle Winery

feel deflated, discouraged, and distressed about producing such perfection. I have seen anxiety and even tears associated with trying to meet such standards during the planning stages of a wedding and, worse, during the actual wedding day.

It does not have to be this way.

My best advice in how to avoid planning stress is to theme your wedding and then to use a checklist to put all your decisions through the lens of that theme. Taking this approach simplifies decision making. Couples can choose a few outstanding details to make their theme shine and their wedding plans will come together comfortably, without all the drama. To channel you down one easy, tasty, and elegant path, I propose you choose a wine wedding theme.

What Is a Wine Wedding?

A wine wedding incorporates wine as a main ingredient in all wedding-related decisions—not merely as a beverage. In a wine-themed wedding, couples choose color schemes inspired by wineries or vineyards, select décor and attire with wine flourishes, such as cork or wine-themed jewelry. They incorporate wine into the cocktail hour and food menu in unique ways, and perhaps even host the wedding at a winery or vineyard. During the wedding ceremony, couples may choose to perform a wine unification ceremony or present readings that reference vineyards, Mother Nature, or winemaking as metaphors for marriage. The idea is that every aspect of your wedding, from the ceremony to florals to menus and décor, centers around winery and vineyard touches.

Wine weddings are timeless and elegant. Wine has been around for thousands of years and will be around for thousands more. It is universally regarded as a culinary wonder that, if chosen correctly, makes excellent food taste even better. A wine theme provides a natural color palate that blends seamlessly with your chosen venue. Imagine a wine color scheme of burgundy and green set against the backdrop of a

Amy's Personal Wedding Journey

For my wedding, I shortened the planning time to less than six months! Engaged on Valentine's Day in February, Cesar and I wed on September 2. I felt the quick timeframe would leave less room for anticipation anxiety and force us to make simple, quick decisions.

A vineyard naturally frames the bride and groom. *K. Lenox Photography*

vineyard in the fall! (I will present this and many other possible color combinations in the next chapter to get your imagination moving.) Wine-based menus will make your cocktail hour a delight and your dinner menu memorable. Picture a cocktail hour where your guests enjoy a specialty wine-based cocktail such as a Seyval Blanc Cranberry Margarita (especially fun if it hints at your honeymoon in Mexico!), or a dinner menu with Wine Barrel-Smoked Salmon and Beef Tenderloin in a Red Wine Sauce. The endlessly awesome choices for wine favors, wine décor, and other special touches for your wedding will leave guests with special memories for years to come. In the coming pages, I share with you all my tips, tricks, and stories from weddings past (including my own) that will aid you in planning the best wedding for you!

A good wedding, like a good marriage, is the result of a hundred choices that come together cohesively.

CHOOSING A WINE THEME—WHY THEME YOUR WEDDING? 9

My wish for you is that once you choose a timeless wine theme, your wedding will be much easier to plan. You will feel in control and not stressed. And, as a result, you will throw the wedding of your dreams and want to bask in the beautiful memories forever. Having run all your decision making through the lens of a wine theme will make the days leading up to your wedding that much easier!

AMY'S FAVORITE TOUCHES

Consider sending a wine-themed save-the-date announcement. You can custom label tiny wine bottles with your names and the date of your wedding, tucking more details, such as travel information, inside the bottles. These will need to be mailed in a box and require more postage, but there will be no question what your theme is!

Let's get right to it! First, I'll help you nail down your specific wine theme by guiding you through certain questions that will solidify your goals, wishes, and dreams into a solid plan, and then I'll suggest color schemes to get the wheels spinning. Then, we'll think about the perfect venue (which doesn't necessarily have to be a vineyard or winery) before covering everything from wedding attire, to favors, to décor, to cocktail hour and food menus. We'll even discuss post-wedding details, such as the perfect thank-you note. I've got you covered! Let's get started.

Dachowski Photography

Anthony Thornton Photography

K. Lenox Photography

Heather Donald Photography

CHAPTER TWO

Creating a Wine Wedding Theme and Color Scheme

I invite you now to think about the big picture and your theme. Your wedding requires an overall vision, and that is where we should start. For this process, you must ask yourself the tough questions about budget, vision, location, timing, and theme.

The budget may be the overall driving factor, so it is important to work that out early because it will steer many other decisions. Who will pay for the wedding? Will any relatives contribute? Or, if you're footing the bill, how long will it take you to save for the wedding you want?

Once you know your budget, consider whether you have a certain type of wedding in mind. When you close your eyes, do you imagine yourself in a huge, fluffy wedding dress with loads of bridesmaids in a garden setting where three hundred of your friends and relatives are gathered? Or do you see a small celebration by the sea? Do you long for a formal affair with a multi-course dinner and tall glistening candelabras gracing every table, or would you rather have a casual backyard event or barbecue? I encourage you to find the authentic expression of your heart's desire for your wedding day, and then bring it to fruition through your choices.

Consider your timing as well. How quickly would you like to be married? Are there lifestyle considerations, such as job moves, plans to start a family, or travel that will impact your timeline? Are there certain relatives or friends who simply must be there and whose circumstances you should also consider?

With an overall picture in mind, now is the right time to choose a theme for your wedding. I, of course, suggest you make it a wine wedding!

Say, for example, in your dreamiest of wedding dreams you choose to have a backyard, at-home wedding. Awesome! With a wine theme to guide you, you can make your event memorable and amazing. First, you can pick a color scheme that reminds guests of wine and vineyards. Next, you could incorporate grapevine and wine-colored flowers in your floral arrangements. Your décor could consist of rented wine barrels to be used as cocktail tables (so much better than those awful plastic tables!). You could let guests know where they will be sitting using cork place cards. The table centerpieces could feature wine bottles with table numbers and cork garlands. Cocktail hour planning would be a cinch with wine cocktails based on the season, and your menu could reflect wine as a main ingredient in all the dishes made by your caterer.

A wine-themed wedding leaves room for much flexibility but streamlines your decisions. Take a peek at the checklist at the end of this book, which is an at-a-glance guide to planning a wine wedding. With these decisions settled and the checklist in hand, your event planning can be easy!

How Color Evokes Certain Emotions

Marketing professionals and other experts have long used color to convey specific ideas and thoughts about a brand's products and services. Think Coca-Cola and its vibrant red, which is meant to convey fun, or Whole Foods, with its browns and greens to convey their earth-friendly approach.

Some colors evoke sadness (grey) and others happiness (orange). Colors can evoke feelings that sway the perceiver in one direction or another. For example, blue can set a tranquil mood (and is used in many bank logos for that reason), and red or orange is more energizing. Green is typically associated with envy. In every way and everything you see, color conveys emotion. The same will be true in your color selections for your wedding. You can craft the entire look and feel of your event and drive your guests' perception of it through proper color selection.

Consider the color chart to the right and the emotions connected to each color. For example, a luxury brand might choose black and gold to express elegance, high price, and exclusivity. An American company might choose red, white, and blue to convey their patriotism.

Likewise,, you can "brand" your wedding by choosing specific colors that will convey your theme so guests know how to think and feel about your celebration.

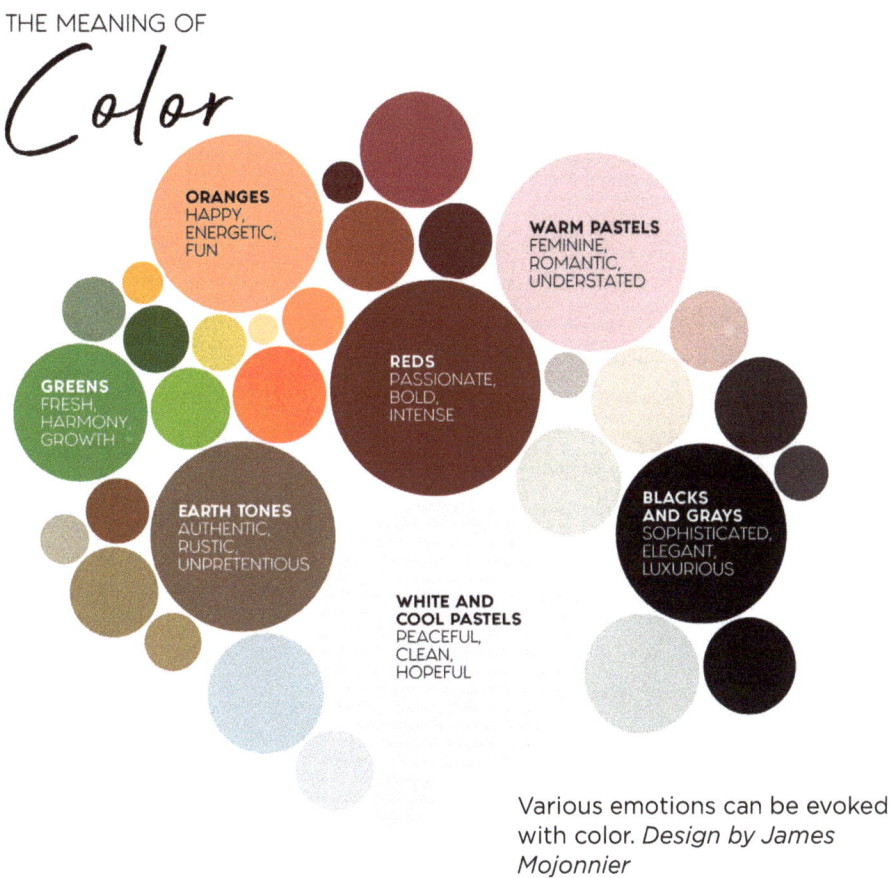

Various emotions can be evoked with color. *Design by James Mojonnier*

You may also wish to start thinking of it as you would a business, with budget, marketing and communication plans, a website, and a product (the wedding!). "Brand" colors will help give your wedding a certain vibe.

Vision Boarding Your Wedding

What is your personal color palette? To what colors are you drawn? What colors do you like to wear or use to decorate your home? These favorite colors can help you zero in on your wedding palette. Small personal touches to showcase your individual style are the key to creating memorable weddings. Collecting all these elements in one place, such as on a vision board, will be crucial to the success of your overall vision.

AMY'S FAVORITE TOUCHES

Many make-your-own tools exist to create a simple website to showcase your wedding details, photos, and more. Wix is one such website tool that is easy to use!

I strongly suggest you visit a fabric store and settle in for a while. There, you will find hues and textures that may inspire you. Pay attention to the colors and fabrics to which you are drawn. At the fabric store, purchase a small length of your favorites. Be sure to also check out the trim and ribbon sections. With these samples in hand, you can begin to build your Wine Wedding Vision Board.

A wedding vision board is a collection of items that begin to build the entire picture and plan for your wedding day. This may be done with actual samples that you can touch and feel (if you are old school like me) or you can build it

electronically on a site such as Pinterest, which offers you the ability to pin photos in groupings as needed. I like to see the samples in person because I worry the online versions will not accurately convey the true look and feel I'm going for.

If making a physical vision board, you can use a cork board or similar board that will accept pushpins or staples, or you can cover a heavy-duty piece of cardboard with neutral paper and use tape to build your collage. You may also wish to use a shallow tray to hold items such as fabric samples and bulkier items. The basic idea is to put every element, color, texture, fabric, and photo that expresses your desires and wishes in one place to keep your wedding focused and on theme. This way, you can see all your choices in one spot, which will give you the overall look and feel of the event.

> *Amy's Personal Wedding Journey*
>
> When I visited a fabric store while planning my wedding, sage greens and copper metallics kept catching my eye and heart. I was also drawn to the texture of burlap for its timeless but unstuffy elegance.

To fill out your wine wedding vision board even further, you should also grab a few bridal magazines and cut out pictures that speak to you. These could include dresses you like, table décor ideas, men's wear that catches your eye, and other small touches you will incorporate into your wedding plan. You could even include a picture of your honeymoon destination! It's important to note that your initial vision board is a starting point, and it will evolve. As you narrow your wedding dress choices down to one, for example, you can remove all other dress photos and just include "The One" dreamy dress, and so on.

◀ Creating a vision board helps you see the big picture. *James Mojonnier*

CREATING A WINE WEDDING THEME AND COLOR SCHEME   17

AMY'S FAVORITE TOUCHES

You might consider international or ethnic elements as part of your wine theme, which might inform your color choices. For example, if you are Italian, your wedding could showcase Italian wine and food, which would in turn influence the décor, menu, beverages, and color schemes. I imagine an Italian grazing table with cheeses and antipasti; large chianti bottles dripping with candles; and prosecco-inspired cocktails accented with greens, reds, and whites. Or maybe you love all things French! How about a reception featuring black, white, and pink with "La Vie En Rose" playing in the background while guests enjoy crepes and sip French 75 cocktails made with gin and champagne?

Choosing Your Color Scheme

Choosing your color scheme should feel natural and should express who you are as a couple and what you love, and should mesh with your chosen venue. For example, for wine weddings at the winery, we like to see color schemes that blend naturally with wine production, wine barrels, oak, vineyards, grapes, touches of iron, aluminum, or stainless steel. I let color and texture dictate the design of the event and find that it often influences the choices for venue and ceremony site. It is best to choose two dominant colors with a possible third accenting color and to also have two textural elements.

Consider the following color combinations as inspiration, all of which impeccably incorporate a wine theme and also achieve the important goal of ensuring the bride is in the spotlight.

Barrels, Burgundy, and Cream

This color and textural combination asserts a seriousness, elegance, and certain heft to your event. You could rent wine barrels for the décor; they work wonderfully as cocktail tables when topped with a glass round. The brushed aluminum of the barrel rings can be introduced as an accent color to your save-the-date announcements, wedding invitations, or thank-you notes. Bridesmaid dresses are readily available in burgundy. And, for this color combination, I see the bride in light cream, blending elegantly with the other tones.

Design by James Mojonnier

Green Grapes, Cream, and Wrought Iron

Green and cream together convey the freshness of a garden or vineyard wedding. A white bridal gown and table linens set off this crisp color palate, while green could be used in custom-made or rented table runners and napkins, in bridesmaid dresses, and in décor. Grape leaves could accent the tables and underlay the center décor and could be added to flowers. Incorporate the feeling of an iron garden gate by installing one to flank the bride's ceremony entrance. Search flea or antiques markets for such gates. I have had luck finding these at the famous Brimfield Flea Market and Antique Shows in Brimfield, Massachusetts.

Design by James Mojonnier

Sparkles, Black, and Stainless

These colors and elements together will help you pull off a champagne-themed wedding, suitable for a black-tie, elegant affair. You could have a lot of fun with this theme, designing invitations with bubbles (or the suggestion of them), and silver and gold balloons in your décor. Black linens set off with glitzy napkins and table décor with sparkly elements would surely dazzle your guests, who you might ask to dress in cocktail or black-tie apparel. A fancy affair is also a great excuse to hire a big band for your reception.

Design by James Mojonnier

Greens, Burgundy, Twine, and Burlap

The elements in the ensemble pictured here convey a farm look and feel and can lend a comfortable, laid-back vibe to your event. A more refined burlap makes for a beautiful table runner, and burlap wrapped loosely around centerpiece bases or plants in the room is also a nice touch. Florals in burgundy and deep reds with fresh green bursts are stunning and multi-seasonal. Burlap tied with twine may also be used to wrap the backs of chairs. Twine-tied napkins are lovely. With this ensemble, cream or white linens will work well, but this should be decided when the dress is chosen. If a pure white bridal gown is worn, I'd suggest pure white linens.

Design by James Mojonnier

Design by James Mojonnier

Autumn Leaves and Barrels

This wine wedding color theme suggests vibrancy, fun, and intensity, and makes for stunning photos. To me, this theme begins with florals in rich tones for the bridal party as well as on the tables. I once saw a bride wrap door casings in florals and the result was stunning. These vivacious colors suggest happiness! Touches of orange or tangerine could be used as a pop of color on save-the-date announcements and, again, on the wedding invitations and thank-you notes.

Pastels and Mercury Glass

White is the first color we associate with weddings for obvious reasons, and a winter white wedding is spectacular. Think of the gorgeous fur-collared cape you can wear over your gown! Velvets can be set off with soft, barely-there pinks, while antique-looking mercury glass votives and vases create a warm feel. Lace works well in this color combination and can be incorporated into your cake design, invitations, table décor, or dresses.

Design by James Mojonnier

Red and Blush Wine

A wine-themed wedding demands wine-themed colors, and this color combination is a knockout! Natural and soft, these choices will never go out of style. Florals to match will be a dream. With this color combination, I envision a bride in a cream or champagne-hued dress, or possibly the barest of blushes in one layer of the skirt. Glass elements are important to incorporate here, as are oak and brushed metals.

Design by James Mojonnier

Design by James Mojonnier

Buttercream, Roses, and Sage

The color sage is so grounding and is one I used in my wedding, with copper and blush accents. In this palette, you can spray paint clay pots copper for décor, or use copper-toned lanterns filled with cork surrounding centerpiece candles. Weddings should have candles everywhere. Adorn chairs with sage-colored fabric, and accent florals with blush roses tucked into the chair décor and bouquets. The bridal gown can lean toward a buttercream hue with copper or deep gold highlights on the shoe and other small details. These colors work so well for an outdoor ceremony, too, with sage and blush florals adorning an arbor.

Design by James Mojonnier

Chocolate and Roses

One of my favorite weddings at LaBelle Winery was all chocolate brown and soft rose hues. The bridesmaids wore the barest breath of rose. Their dresses were almost cream. In contrast, rich chocolate linens set a beautiful tableau for soft roses in low bouquets wrapped in refined burlap. Welcome gifts and favors can be chocolate and wine-themed, tied with soft pink ribbons—a great combination for spring weddings transitioning from winter with a nod toward the growing season ahead. Choosing your color scheme will make all other decisions easier, including where to host your main event, which we'll discuss in the next chapter.

CHAPTER THREE

Selecting a Venue and Ceremony Site

A wine-themed wedding presents so many options for where to hold your ceremony and celebration (and there are many choices other than the obvious vineyard or winery). The setting of your wedding plays a huge role in establishing your overall look and feel. But first things first: to choose a venue, you have to look into your heart and ask yourself what your overall vision for your wedding day really is.

First, you must choose the time of day you'd prefer to be wed. Your options include brunch, lunch, or dinner timeframes, and each bring their own special magic.

Morning weddings can be easy on the budget, and the cocktail and menu planning can be creative because—let's face it—who doesn't love brunch? However, getting married early in the day can present a few challenges as well. The early start time requires early wake ups, and hair, nails, dressing, and the like will be at a rapid pace to meet timelines. If you are very prepared and somewhat low maintenance, the early hour won't present too much of a problem. Consider planning your rehearsal the day before as a luncheon or very early mid-afternoon celebration so you can wrap up early enough for an early bedtime.

Another option is an afternoon wedding with either a casual or formal luncheon. Picture a large luncheon picnic setting for something different, unexpected, and unique. This works well if your heart's desire is to marry by the sea. Think about the fun you could have if you spread out picnic blankets and rented picnic tables, all set with picnic wine and beautiful baskets brimming with cheese, bread, and charcuterie, of course. Lawn games could be set out for guests to amuse themselves during cocktail hour, and children can blend seamlessly into events such as this.

Still, the majority of couples prefer the traditional, formal affair of a late afternoon wedding and evening celebration. This remains our most popular option at LaBelle Winery, as it seems most suited to a multi-course dinner, a live band (if that's your preference), and loads of dancing and celebration!

Part of your decision may be driven by your ceremony preferences. Will you be married in a church or other faith-based location? Do you prefer to be married outside under the big, blue sky or inside to control the elements? Does your religion or culture require that certain traditions be upheld? Choose a ceremony location, and the rest of your decisions can flow from that.

Once you've decided the time of day and whether your ceremony will be at a venue or off-site, you should begin to visit venues that strike your fancy and, if you've decided to plan a wine-themed wedding, you have some obvious choices (a winery) and some not-so-obvious choices.

Winery and Vineyard Weddings

If you've decided on a wine-themed wedding, getting married at a winery is the most obvious choice! At a winery and vineyard, there are so many attributes and bonus offerings that will make your theme effortless to achieve.

> **Amy's Personal Wedding Journey**
>
> I opted for a morning ceremony in a garden, followed by a brunch. A brunch wedding can be formal or casual and is often a little easier on the budget. My husband and I were also planning to build a house when we got married and were paying for our own wedding, so we wanted to keep costs under control. Plus, I love the cocktail and food options for brunch. My favorite food from my wedding was a brûléed grapefruit, served at a fruit station. The idea of being married in September's morning light was alluring to me.

All four seasons in the life of the vineyard are depicted here.
LaBelle Winery

Your ceremony can be outside in the vineyard or another location on the grounds of the winery. The natural beauty of the perfectly laid rows of a vineyard offers stunning backdrops for your ceremony and photos. In the spring, the vineyard offers tiny budding bunches of green grapes. During the late summer months, the grape clusters enter *veraison*, a time when red grapes turn red and white wine grapes turn golden green. This is also when grapes begin to turn sweet. Of course, in fall, we enter harvest time, when the grape bunches hang lusciously from the bottom canes of the vines, heavy with juice and sugar and waiting to be turned into wine. The leaves of the grapevines in the fall begin to show some signs of stress and display fall colors and tones. Taking these color and tonal changes

This wedding ceremony overlooked the vineyard. *K. Lenox Photography*

into account will be important to your overall theme and color scheme.

Hopefully you can find a winery and vineyard that also offers an outdoor terrace or wine cellar option for your cocktail hour. At LaBelle Winery, our couples often have their ceremony on the Vineyard Overlook, which literally overlooks the myriad rows and rows of vines. A winery cocktail hour needs to have vines in view.

Winery locations also often have a celebration venue to accommodate the reception. This may be an outside location under a tent or indoors.

When considering tented, outdoor venues, you should think about the weather and seasonality. Of course, you can easily extend shoulder seasons in such spaces with heaters, tent sides, and by offering guests wraps and blankets. But ultimately, you want your guests to be comfortable so it's best to keep the weather in mind.

Tents (or other sheltered areas) may be provided by your venue as part of your

AMY'S FAVORITE TOUCHES

Make sure your chosen vineyard has a "Plan B"—a secondary location—in case of inclement weather. Also, check if the venue has other features on site such as a restaurant and tasting room. You'll want to know options for your guests but, more importantly, you'll want to know who else will be on property and circulating when your event is taking place.

rental package, or you may look to rent an appropriate one. When seeking tents for this most special of occasions, I recommend you search for tent companies that provide canvas tents. They look much more elegant than the plastic or vinyl ones. Also, canvas tents typically come with fun accoutrements like flags and multiple peaks. Look carefully at rental company reviews and letters of recommendation because this element of your wedding is foundational and really needs to be spot on.

This vineyard arbor was made of upcycled pieces of oak wine barrels. *Millyard Studios*

AMY'S FAVORITE TOUCHES

There is a new trend of clear tents made from heavy-grade plastic or vinyl that glow when lit with night lighting and allow you to see the stars! They are beautiful, but use caution, as they can get and stay very hot in summer.

A wedding inside a winery will usually have a casual elegance and style. As you lean into your wine wedding theme, you'll want to pick a spot at the winery for the reception that can both accommodate your guests and integrate your theme perfectly. For example, the winery itself, with its tanks and barrels, might be a suitable space to host a memorable event for your family and friends. Consideration must be given to the temperature, as such spaces are often chilly and damp. If so, note this to guests in advance or provide wraps that fit into your color scheme.

Your venue may offer a formal dining space or great hall, as LaBelle Winery does. Though the venue may be gorgeous unadorned, consider whether you need to add wine barrels or other décor. The large beams overhead at LaBelle Winery, for example, offer a perfect setup for hanging planks, lights, flowers, or draping to add additional pizazz (we will dive into this more in Chapter 5).

A personal welcome sign is a nice touch and makes your guests feel special. *Millyard Studios*

Using Other Venues for Wine Weddings

Just because you are throwing a wine-themed wedding does not mean you must have your wedding at a winery! There are beautiful, unique wedding venues everywhere, from churches, parks, beaches, libraries, country clubs, hotels, inns, museums, botanical gardens, to backyards. A wine-themed wedding can enhance any of these options.

If you're having a wine-themed wedding at a venue other than a winery or vineyard, you'll need to ensure that your décor, cocktail selections, menu choices, and other touches drive home the theme.

Infusing a venue with a wine theme could begin with renting wine barrels for cocktail tables, using farm-style cross-back chairs for dining, or barrel-toned wood accents for signage ("Ceremony this way!"), and the like. Florals should be kept in line with vineyard and wine color schemes, and should include grape leaves wherever possible. Cork accents are a must in this case, and buying used corks online or from a local winery will enable you to make many cork-based décor items (as discussed in Chapter 5).

> **Amy's Personal Wedding Journey**
>
> My wedding venue was an historic inn. We included wine that I made as a favor to guests, offered a wine-infused chocolate fountain for dessert, and had our ceremony outside in the garden. Guests who were staying at the inn received welcome baskets with wine and cheese, examples of which you'll see later in this book.

Your venue will dictate many of your choices. For example, if you choose to have a wine-themed wedding at a beach, you'll want to consider setting up an aisle and "altar" with wine barrels and maybe a grapevine arch. Aisles could be formed with cork garlands or simple hanging plant stakes, adorned with hearts made out of cork, all strung together. Cocktail hour could find your guests with a glass of Sauvignon Blanc or a Riesling Basil Mojito, nibbling on wine-infused appetizers.

Consider the layout of your ceremony chairs as well. There is no rule that states you must have straight rows, two aisles, and a church-like setting (unless you are actually in a church with stationary seating).

For example, your ceremony chairs could be set in two sections, with a center aisle, in a semi-circular pattern. By doing this, guests can feel closer to the wedding couple and have a better vantage point. After all, they can't wait to see you and your beloved ready to embark on your new marriage journey!

AMY'S FAVORITE TOUCHES

One chair setup I loved was an entire circle set with four aisles to break it up. The wedding couple entered to the center of the circle, surrounded by people who loved them. In this setup, everyone had a very good view of the ceremony. The bride's father built a doorway with French doors for her to enter through, signifying her entrance into her new life. It was symbolic and magical.

Heather Donald Photography

The chairs for this vineyard wedding were laid out in a circular pattern. *Millyard Studios*

Of course, the traditional setup of chairs in two sections and a center aisle is still great because it works well. Your room or location may dictate just how much creativity you can have in this regard, but I encourage you to think outside the box when designing your room or ceremony layout.

Now that you've decided where you are getting married, you can turn your attention to the details of your bridal party attire and welcoming your guests. Read on and be inspired to create a beautiful, seamless event that incorporates wine at every step.

CHAPTER FOUR

Dressing the Bridal Party and Welcoming Traveling Guests

Now that you have chosen a date, venue, color scheme, and wine as your theme, you are ready to move on to the smaller details, which can add a lot of merriment, joy, and pizzazz to your wedding celebrations. To me, everything is in the details, and it's these tiny things that will put your event over the top and make it outstanding. I take this same approach in my business where, yes, the big picture is so important—the building, the team, the grounds, and so on. But the smaller details such as lighting, temperature, and music really elevate my restaurant.

How to Incorporate a Wine Theme into Your Bridal Party's Attire

Your bridal party can be bedecked in an array of accessories that subtly transmit your wine theme and are also functional and fun. For example, small purses for your bridal party can be found by visiting vintage or antiques stores. They don't necessarily need to be all the same because you can tie them together by customizing them to your color and theme. Let's say you find five cream-toned vintage clutch purses for your bridal attendants and your flower colors are all fall jewel tones. With a hot glue gun and the best quality silk flowers you can find, you could glue on dahlias or other flowers to match your floral theme to tie all the purses together. You could even glue the cut-off end of a cork in the center of the flower.

Fill cork purses for your bridesmaids with goodies. *James Mojonnier*

In addition to being a lovely accessory, you should make the purses functional, too. A nice touch would be to fill each with tissues, lip gloss, pain reliever packets, and breath mints or spray.

Bridesmaids can all wear the same dress, or they can dress in different styles in the same material. Or you may choose tonal differences in dress colors in the same hues. There is no rule of thumb, here, though the 1980s trend of having all your bridesmaids in a different shade of sherbet has, thankfully, passed.

For the men, wine-themed wedding attire can be all black tie for formal affairs, or more casual, trendy suits and ties that can be worn again and again. In either case, be sure the groomsmen attire blends well with the color scheme of the entire affair. I love to see whimsical choices for groomsmen too, and

Bridesmaids don't always need matching-style dresses. *Millyard Studios*

AMY'S FAVORITE TOUCHES

Consider pulling together your groomsmen's outfit with the bridesmaid dress color by including a perfectly colored handkerchief or pocket square. These are smart, useful, and something you do not see every day.

I gravitate toward bowties and suspenders patterned with wine glasses or grapes. Again here, there are no rules.

Remembrance bracelets or pins are an emotional and beautiful touch. To accomplish this, the wedding couple wears either a charm bracelet or pin inside a jacket with photos of immediate family or close friends who have passed.

For the bride and groom, consider wine-themed accents, such as wine-colored shoes or socks for the gentleman, and wine-colored satin shoes for the bride. Florals, including boutonniéres, can also incorporate a wine theme with grapevine, grape leaves, and cork accents.

Wine-Themed Accessories

Your wine theme can shine bright in your choices for bridal party accessories. Just a few touches can really make a big difference.

One of my favorite accessories that is easy on the budget are wine socks! They are offered in many different designs, from flying corks, wine corkscrews, to barrels and grapes. Many have phrases on the bottoms such as, "If you are reading this bring me more wine." Groomsmen will appreciate this fun accessory.

Bridal Party Gifts

Your wine-themed wedding offers so many great options for gifts for your wedding party! Your bridal party has done a lot for your wedding, and you should thank them with a memorable gift that lasts and that will always remind them of your special bond.

Jewelry is a great choice if it is something they can all wear on your wedding day. This keeps your bridal party in sync. A necklace, bracelet, or earrings that incorporate your wine theme, such as a wine glass silhouette or a piece that incorporates cork will be a wonderful keepsake. Etsy has a plethora of handcrafted items that would be perfect for this purpose in all price ranges. For the gentlemen,

Special remembrances of loved ones pinned to florals are meaningful.
Millyard Studios

Wine-themed socks make dressing fun!
James Mojonnier

I've also seen watches with faces made from wine barrel oak offered online from specialty watch makers.

Personalized wine accessories, such as champagne chillers, corkscrews, wine carriers, wine racks, barrel staves and barrel tops, or decanters are also useful gifts that will always remind your bridal party of your wedding day. Here again, Etsy offers a wide range of gift items from small, artisan producers, but there is an abundance of other websites offering all manner of wine gift ideas. Personalizing these with your bridal attendants' names or, instead, with your wedding date or particular inspirational phrase will be so appreciated.

Another thought is to gift a more expensive or rarer bottle of wine that the bridal party might not readily purchase for themselves. If choosing this option, I strongly encourage you to buy gold-toned permanent markers with which you can write a personal message and the date of your wedding on each bottle, so that when they enjoy it, they will remember your special day and perhaps keep the bottle itself. Or, if you are holding your wedding at a winery, ask the winery to custom bottle the perfect gift for your wedding party with a special label to mark the day and your message of thanks.

If you're gifting bottles of wine or champagne, consider adding monogrammed glassware to match the gift—that is, wine glasses appropriate to the wine or champagne flutes for champagne. High-end glassware can be found at Riedel or Tiffany & Co., or you can find websites offering personalization of these as well.

Wine club services are yet another great gift idea to remind your bridal party how much you appreciate them. If you are getting married at a winery, a nice touch is to join the winery's wine club in the name of your bridal attendants so that they can receive monthly or quarterly mailings of wine from your special place. Many wineries offer this service and, if yours does not, you can find wine clubs online that specialize in wine gifting.

Welcome Baskets

Speaking of gifts, let's not forget the awesome people in your life who have traveled from afar to take part in your big day! I think it is so important to not only welcome them to the area but to also make them comfortable by showing them a bit of hospitality. One great way to do this is to place welcome baskets for them at the hotel so that, upon arrival, they immediately feel included, welcome, and involved.

What's best to offer in these baskets? Here again, the wine theme rescues you and makes this an easy task to accomplish. A wine-themed welcome basket can be an actual basket or a nice-looking gift bag, or, my personal favorite, a mini crate. Crinkle-cut paper enhances the look, but you can certainly use other basket fillers. You can find crinkle-cut paper online or in craft stores.

A bottle of wine makes a unique and appreciated thank-you for your bridal party.
James Mojonnier

So many wonderful options exist for filling these welcome baskets! Of course, we start with a nice bottle of wine. The wine does not need to be expensive and should be a light wine, perhaps white, that's easy to drink on its own without food. I

> ### Amy's Personal Wedding Journey
>
> Since I didn't get married until I was thirty-five, I opted to ask my friends to participate in my wedding day through ceremony readings or in performing other special jobs. I did not have adults in my wedding party, and instead, I asked all my friends and family's little girls to stand up with me and it was delightful! Bedecked in creamy white ankle-length gowns with sage organza belts and ballet slippers, they looked like angels (until they attacked the chocolate fountain, most of which ended up on their dresses!)

recommend a Pinot Grigio, Seyval Blanc, or Sauvignon Blanc for this purpose. Or, you could opt for bubbly, which is always a hit and strikes a nice, celebratory tone.

To this, add glasses that are appropriate to the wine chosen. Depending on your budget, these can be standard or high end, personalized or plain. You'll also need to provide a corkscrew, which could be personalized with your wedding date or a welcome message as well. Or, buy a plain corkscrews and tie a tag with a welcome message to them with brown twine and kraft paper.

Welcome baskets should also include a list of area highlights and fun things to do or area restaurants that guests should not miss, if time permits. Even one recommendation to a local bakery with extraordinary muffins or bread will be appreciated.

Baskets should also include cheese and crackers, in keeping with your wine theme. For this, I recommend high end artisan crackers and hard cheeses. Charcuterie with grainy mustard is also a nice touch, but remember to include a knife if anything needs to be cut. Bonus points if you can include fresh fruit, such as figs or grapes and apples as well. You may need to enlist the help of a bridal attendant to accomplish this last-minute task of adding fresh fruit.

Top these baskets with a hand-written note expressing your excitement that your guests could join you for your wedding celebration and thanking them for traveling. Your guests will so appreciate this gesture and it will set the mood for the intimate celebration to come.

So, you've decided how you will dress your bridal party in great wine style and welcome guests with yummy wine-themed treats. Now it's time to focus on decorating your wedding in wine style. In the next chapter, you'll get some great ideas on how to really elevate your wine theme and adorn your wedding ceremony and reception with wine-focused décor.

Welcome your traveling guests in taste and style with a thoughtfully created gift basket (or crate!). *James Mojonnier*

K. Lenox Photography

CHAPTER FIVE

Creating Unique Wine-Themed Décor

Creating a unique décor for your wine-themed wedding will be an adventure of the imagination! There are so many options within this category, you will have to restrain yourself from overdoing it or selecting too many avenues to go down, or you'll risk cluttering your event with sensory overload. Strive for an elegant, refined inclusion of your wine theme, rather than overt, in-your-face excess. The old adage "a little goes a long way" applies well here.

I applied this same restraint in designing my winery tasting room. Rather than feature *everything* winery, I chose a classic, timeless architectural style and wove in subtle winery nuances. For example, the chandeliers in the LaBelle Winery Tasting Room are made from deconstructed wine barrel parts—staves and rings—but they offer just the *suggestion* of a wine barrel in their design rather than being an actual barrel. I have used these chandeliers in the LaBelle Winery Market as well.

Let's take a look at some elegant, useful ways you could include wine-themed décor into your wedding celebration.

Seating Arrangements and Table Décor

I love it when décor is functional. The fact is, you need a way to number or otherwise mark your tables so guests know where they should sit. You will also need a corresponding seating chart or place cards noted with the assigned table. The staff at your venue will need this information well in advance so they can plan for appropriate table layouts and seating arrangements. Check with your venue and

I wove subtle wine references into the décor of the LaBelle Winery Tasting Room. *LaBelle Winery*

A windowpane seating chart is an attractive way to inform guests where you have placed them. *Millyard Studios*

sales representative to see if they can share their seating chart options with you, and be sure to inquire about the size of their standard tables. This is important information so you can figure out whether you can fit eight, ten, or twelve people per table. Of course, if you do not like the tables that are offered, you are welcome to rent according to your heart's desire. Also be sure to preview the seats and linens to ensure you like the style. If you do not like the chairs, rental chair covers are an option and are often offered with embellishments.

AMY'S FAVORITE TOUCHES

At LaBelle Winery, we like to use antique mirrors or antique windows with nine or twelve panes as seating charts, using each pane to represent one table. Somehow, antique items and the winery theme go hand in hand. We have also used a large, framed board filled with corks as a literal cork board upon which to pin place cards.

When guests arrive at the reception space after cocktail hour, they will immediately need to know where they are sitting. They will want to put down their accessories and coats and get ready to enjoy the party! It's best to offer this information to your guests in an organized and efficient fashion. My favorite way is to incorporate corks as place-card holders by cutting small slits in the corks and inserting the place cards. Another option is to create a large, hand-lettered seating chart.

Champagne cork place-card holders carry the wine theme to the reception. *Millyard Studios*

Once guests know their table, they will need to be able to find it easily. There are many options to incorporate a wine theme into the table markers. My favorite is to place a beautifully printed label with the table number on a wine bottle. These are especially beautiful when the couple inserts fairy lights in the bottle, as they create a romantic glow that augments the candlelight. I have also seen table number cards inserted in the corks of wine bottles, or bottles that have been spray painted a shimmering gold and marked with the table number for dramatic effect. Or use little groupings of cork tied with twine to hold 5x7 cardstock with a calligraphy or painted number to designate a table. Some couples choose to make table numbers out of cork with some hot glue, die-cut frames purchased from an arts and crafts store, and a little elbow grease (and maybe a bottle of wine while working on them!).

This table scape offers intimate conversation as well as elegant flare. *Heather Donald Photography*

Wine bottles make great table numbers. *K. Lenox Photography*

Of course, you are not limited to numbering your tables. For a wine-themed wedding, I think it is creative to name tables after wine regions or types. For example, for a two-hundred-person wedding with approximately twenty tables, you'd need twenty table names. Consider selecting from this list:

- Champagne
- Cabernet Sauvignon
- Pinot Grigio
- Pinot Noir
- Seyval Blanc
- Petit Verdot
- Sauvignon Blanc
- Merlot
- Chardonnay
- Chenin Blanc
- Prosecco
- Cava
- Fume Blanc
- Rose
- Zinfandel
- Riesling
- Gewurztraminer
- Tokai
- Saki
- Chianti
- Barolo
- Super Tuscan
- Lambrusco
- Moscato
- Malbec
- Tempranillo

This wine-themed table setting is so elegant. *Millyard Studios*

Whatever you decide to do, keep in mind that a little goes a long way and subtlety is often your friend. Here are some other ideas to incorporate your wine theme in a functional way.

Cork Décor

Décor made with cork is an easy way to highlight your wine theme as well. First, consider whether you will present menus to each guest at each place setting. If doing so, you should note the wine accompanying each course, if any, as well as the food courses. The menu itself can become a keepsake if you include headings such

Have guests sign a wine barrel that you can preserve and keep as memorable home décor. *LaBelle Winery*

as "The Wedding Feast of Amy and Cesar Arboleda" and the date. There are menu backers made of cork that have corners into which you can slip your cardstock menu. Or you might use a wax seal with your monogram to affix the menu to the backer. Wax seals may be customized and purchased on Etsy. Another option is to use a stained oak backer and twine to affix a single menu for every table. Stained oak blends beautifully with a wine theme.

Cork décor can be incorporated into your ceremony and throughout your reception. I've seen couples use corks to create their initials or monogram, which they set on the bar as décor. Others have used corks to create hanging hearts, wreaths, baskets, floral bases, and display bases for photos of the wedding couple.

With a little bit of creativity and a large bag of used corks (from a lot of wine drinking!), you can make some lovely accents for your celebration. Just remember to not go overboard!

Guest Books

Your wine theme may also be on display in your guest book choice. Ditching the traditional guest book, many LaBelle Winery couples choose barrel tops that they later seal with polyurethane to preserve their guests' signatures (or they use the entire barrel, see below).

AMY'S FAVORITE TOUCHES

LaBelle Winery menus are draped in a cork material and branded with my logo, subtly bringing in the wine theme. Menu backers made of cork for your table display can be found at many online stores.

AMY'S FAVORITE TOUCHES

One of my favorite trends is to place a video recorder or smartphone on the guest book table and ask guests to film a quick message to you. These can be touching and hilarious and are a wonderful way to document your celebration. You could also provide a few Polaroid cameras and ask guests to snap candid photos and then write messages on the bottom or back of each.

Other couples have had guests sign three bottles of LaBelle Wine, one for their first-year, one for their third-year, and one for their fifth-year anniversary. They can then enjoy these bottles years later and remember their special day.

Wine Barrels

Wine barrels can serve as very functional décor! If your venue does not have them on hand, you can typically rent them from an events company or winery for your wedding celebration.

> *Amy's Personal Wedding Journey*
>
> Cesar and I created "fun facts" about our relationship, families, and backgrounds and placed these on the tables in a little stack of cards, printed on paper that matched our invitations. We thought it would be fun for guests to get to know us more intimately with trivia such as "Cesar's father has 22 siblings!"

I love to see barrels topped with cascading florals flanking a couple at the ceremony site. They set the scene and provide a focal point for gorgeous pictures. These can be functional, too, as props for a wine unity ceremony can be placed on top of the barrels, out of sight if need be. (I'll explain more on wine unity ceremonies in Chapter 7.) In addition, you could purchase one to serve as your guest book! Have guests sign the barrel with messages of love and then repurpose that wine barrel as a table in your home by using a glass top.

Wine barrels make great cocktail tables when topped with glass tabletops, which may be purchased online. At LaBelle Winery, we fit barrels with locking casters so they can easily be moved during parties. They set a nice tone, and they are a great height for cocktail hour.

Wine barrels decorate your ceremony beautifully. *Millyard Studios*

> ### Amy's Personal Wedding Journey
>
> For our wedding, Cesar and I used a blank canvas, and asked people to sign it with metallic markers. This treasure hangs in our home to this day. To make this idea a wine theme, you could mount a canvas in a cork frame.

Your wedding cake can also be gorgeous displayed on a wine barrel table a with glass topper. The barrel height is perfect as a cake table and a great way to incorporate your wine theme. Make sure the barrel isn't tipsy, as cakes can weigh a lot, and you wouldn't want it to fall over!

Another use for wine barrels is as a dessert display or late-night snacks display or buffet. To accomplish this, place a long live-edge wooden plank across two barrels. Then, decorate with different elevations of plates and platters, candles, and florals. Often, the bridal party florals in vases can be used for this purpose.

Wine Favors

Though not required, it is customary to place a small gift at each place setting to welcome your guests to the reception and to express gratitude for their attendance at your wedding. In a wine wedding, you have so many options for this gift to include your theme.

I love to see a wine jam or jelly with a cute note attached in twine. Your venue may be willing to make these, or you could find a local jam producer and contract with them for a small batch. Or, if you are talented in the kitchen or have family members who are, wine jams are not too difficult to make at home.

A corkscrew can be customized in myriad colors and styles as a nice thank-you gift with the date of your wedding. Or you may wish to share a bottle of wine as a favor, perhaps customized with your own label. Many companies offer this service online. In this case, only one bottle per couple is required. Of course, single guests should receive a full bottle.

Overall, incorporating wine décor into your theme and celebration will tie together all the other wine-themed details of your wedding day.

With your décor strongly rooted in your wine theme, you are now ready to plan your rehearsal dinner. In the next chapter, I guide you through the entire process to plan a successful wedding rehearsal that leaves you prepared and excited for your big day!

Wine jelly makes a lovely wedding favor. *James Mojonnier*

CHAPTER SIX

Planning a Meaningful Wine-Themed Rehearsal Dinner

A rehearsal dinner is a celebratory event that usually falls immediately after the wedding ceremony rehearsal the day before a wedding. Invitees are typically all family members, the bridal party, and guests who are from out of town, though the official guest list is at the wedding couple's discretion. This celebration provides a time to host a more intimate gathering that helps each family get to know one another and have the opportunity to relax, mingle, and unite before the flurry of the actual wedding day, when conversation time might be more difficult to find.

Planning Basics

Traditionally, the parents of the groom planned and paid for the rehearsal dinner. But, like so many wedding customs of the past, modern-day couples are taking over the planning and financials for these pre-nuptial parties, partly due to the fact that couples now often wait longer to get married and they have careers and lives of their own and no longer need support from family in this way. I usually suggest that modern-day couples follow these planning steps for a perfect, stress-free celebration:

Deciding Who Hosts

Planning options for the rehearsal dinner are wide open! There are no rules and certainly less formality than that of the wedding day itself. First things first: Talk

Wine barrels can be used for wine tastings at a rehearsal dinner. *K. Lenox Photography*

with your family to decide who's hosting. I find it's best to have an open and honest conversation with immediate family members to avoid awkward conversations later. Just ask. It's best, trust me. And a frank conversation about this will help avoid unnecessary wedding stress.

Choosing a Rehearsal Party Theme

Once the issue of hosting is settled, you'll need to decide on a fantastic theme and central controlling idea. My advice is to do something opposite of the wedding theme and feel. If your wedding day will be filled with formality and glamour, go in the reverse direction for the rehearsal dinner and have a super-casual event

AMY'S FAVORITE TOUCHES

At my favorite rehearsal dinner, the couple played a slide show of past family weddings that left a teary and joyful crowd ready to celebrate the next day and usher this new couple into their marriage.

where guests can let their hair down. Think backyard barbeque or barbecue joint, where you can get messy and sit at picnic tables. A house party with a luau or tropical theme to mirror your honeymoon destination could provide loads of fun for guests with scattered Polaroid cameras, tropical drinks with umbrellas, and tropical attire. Casual could also mean a picnic—perhaps in a vineyard or local park—catered with picnic baskets and bottles of wine on blankets. Food trucks have become so popular, and I have seen them used to incredible advantage at a casual backyard rehearsal dinner that requires almost no planning on your part! A carnival theme would be fun with such a choice.

If you are marrying at a winery, a casual rehearsal dinner in the vineyard itself could be stunning and unforgettable. Imagine a long table set for family-style service just as the sun is setting. That's epic. You'll need to consider a Plan B for inclement weather, though, so be sure there is a space into which you may retreat that is different than your reception space. This is key, as you don't want to spoil the surprises of the day to come.

If your wedding will be a casual affair, you may wish to go all out for the rehearsal dinner and make it a cocktail dress and suit kind of night. An excellent restaurant will work well for something fancy and will typically have a private room into which you can recess. Bonus if you can find a hotel venue with a cool rooftop private event space, which sometimes is even available in winter through the magic of modern heating options.

Guests and Invites

Once you've chosen the date and venue, you'll need to decide your final guest list. Family and bridal party members, including those doing readings or performing usher duties, and those who have any part in your ceremony, should be invited to both the ceremony rehearsal and the rehearsal dinner. Anyone staying at a hotel to attend your wedding should also make the list.

Amy's Personal Wedding Journey

At my rehearsal dinner, I gave Tiffany earrings to close friends as I told everyone why they are such amazing people and how much they mean to me.

Formal invitations are not necessary for a rehearsal dinner, unless it's a very formal affair. An online invitation or invite via a website such as Evite will work just fine. However, you still need RSVPs so you have a headcount for your venue. If you have your rehearsal dinner details buttoned up prior to sending out your wedding invitations, it would be nice to include a written invitation in that initial package, but this is not necessary. Invitations to your night-before dinner may be sent six weeks prior at the latest. Your goal here is to be timely and respectful of guests' planning needs.

Most wedding venues will also be hosting a wedding the night before your wedding. As such, they will require you to have your wedding rehearsal in the afternoon, before the room and facility are needed for the other wedding. This is great, because it allows you to get that done and get on to an early dinner so everyone can get to bed early and be refreshed and ready for the big day.

Menu Planning

In planning the rehearsal dinner menu, you can again take your cues from the wedding day and create an event that is totally different. If your wedding will be a three- or four-course formal dinner, think about making your rehearsal dinner a buffet or have food stations or something equally easy and loose. On the contrary,

Cheers! *Cottonbro Studio*

if your wedding reception will be a pig roast, consider a formal menu for the night-before celebration.

If you have a lot of guests traveling from outside the area, a nice touch for the rehearsal dinner is to provide a menu of local favorites. For example, if you are marrying in New England and many people are traveling to celebrate with you, your rehearsal dinner could be seaside and feature a traditional clambake, which typically includes New England clam chowder, Boston baked beans, lobster in all forms, clams, roasted potatoes, and corn on the cob. Serve this with a summer shandy or local wines and beers, and you have a winning theme.

Of course, if you are hosting a wine-themed wedding ceremony and reception, You might want to carry that theme into your rehearsal dinner, which we discuss below.

Toasts and Speeches

It is customary for the host of the rehearsal dinner to welcome guests at the start of the party, and this should be short and sweet. Then, usually a small number of bridal party members or close family give a toast, again short, as this should not replace the formal toasts to come at the reception. The wedding couple themselves (if not the host) should plan to speak briefly as well, thanking bridal party members and their families, in particular their parents if that's appropriate, just before the evening ends. This is a great time for the couple to hand out bridal party gifts and to give any last-minute reminders or instructions regarding activities for the following day.

Wine-Themed Rehearsal Dinner

Now that you know the steps for a perfect rehearsal dinner, let's plan one with some details so I can make this easy for you.

Venue

If you'd like to continue your wine-themed wedding details with the rehearsal dinner planning, you are in luck because this theme will make your planning focused and easy. First, choose a venue. A local winery or vineyard will be perfect, but not necessary. If this is an option, a vineyard picnic or plated dinner would be amazing,

LaBelle Winery wine cellar set for dinner. *LaBelle Winery* ➤

but, even better, can you talk them into letting you host your dinner in their wine cellar? If the space is pretty enough for a dinner, surrounded by glistening tanks that reflect the candlelight perfectly, your guests will never forget your rehearsal. Some wineries also have restaurants attached, and a private room in one of these spaces is also a great choice. At LaBelle Winery, we have a private dining room called The Barrel Room that holds up to fifty people for intimate dining celebrations. Its warmth and cozy atmosphere make for memorable dinners.

Menu Ideas

As discussed previously, I believe your rehearsal dinner menu should contrast with your planned wedding day celebration menu. Casual fun should reign as king at the rehearsal party if you're going formal for the wedding itself. Pitchers of wine-based sangrias and bottles of wine should flow, but not too much, as you have a big day coming up! For this reason, I encourage a beer and wine party only, leaving hard liquor off the menu. This helps keep things lighter and ensures everyone will be in tiptop shape for your wedding day, including you! Sangrias fit the bill nicely, as they provide a lighter alternative to mixed drinks because the fruit juice and ice mixed in lowers the alcohol content.

Sangrias also complement many foods. Imagine a Latin or Mexican fiesta with a taco bar, rice, beans, guacamole, fresh salad, cilantro crema, fresh pico de gallo, and large glass urns or carafes filled with sangria. The décor for these types of parties is simple and festive, and there's sure to be something for everyone to enjoy. Music can set a nice tone here, too, with salsa playing simply off a smartphone playlist, or if your budget allows, a mariachi band!

A wine theme can lean heavily into your heritage as well and be a nice nod to your family and your traditions. For example, an Italian family may opt for an Italian restaurant that serves wines such as Pinot Grigios, Chiantis, Barolos, or Super Tuscans near the venue or hotel where guests are staying. Providing food and wine from your own heritage is an excellent way to showcase who you are and invite your guests to get to know you and your soon-to-be spouse even better.

No matter your choices, above all the rehearsal dinner is a way to bring your families and friends together to enjoy some intimate time before your wedding day.

◀ Guests at a reception table celebrating the happy couple! *Julia Kuzenkov*

CHAPTER SEVEN

Setting the Mood with a Vineyard or Winery Ceremony

A vineyard ceremony can feel particularly special and intimate because inside a vineyard you feel tucked away somehow from the rest of the world in a secret garden all your own. A ceremony inside a winery, perhaps among the barrels of the wine cellar, can feel exclusive, as if you've been allowed into a place you'd never otherwise be. What a wonderful gift to give your guests! In this chapter, we'll dive into the details of planning a beautiful and meaningful wine-themed wedding ceremony.

Vineyard Ceremony

So you are getting married under the big, open sky in a vineyard! How exciting and extraordinary! Let's make a blueprint for complete success. The vineyard location for your ceremony will direct many decisions, some big, such as your choice of readings, and some small, such as shoe choice.

Consider the weather, too. If it will be hot and your guests will be in direct sun, offer a station of fruit-infused waters before your ceremony (see more on this topic in Chapter 8). One LaBelle Winery couple had iced lemonade garnished with mint and served in mason jars available on antique apple-picking ladders for guests to help themselves upon entering the ceremony. Guests may also appreciate

◄ A vineyard ceremony connects you and your guests with nature.
  K. Lenox Photography

AMY'S FAVORITE TOUCHES

If having an outdoor wedding, advise your guests to wear shoes that can travel easily across rocky, gravelly terrain with heels that won't sink into the grass. For some, that means a slipper or flat shoe, even if they change into heels later, once on solid ground. Your guests will appreciate a heads up in the invitation, too, so that they are aware the ceremony will take place outside and can plan accordingly.

Make sure you and your guests wear shoes that don't sink into the grass.
Millyard Studios

beautiful parasols, which can be purchased relatively affordably online, handed out as shade from the sun.

Your ceremony itself should be as unique as your love. Though there are many ways to order your ceremony, I like the following structure best and it is, in fact, what I used for my wedding.

Prelude

During the prelude, as guests arrive and get seated, it is a nice touch to offer music whether recorded or live. Music is so essential, as it carries emotion, memories, and heart. Familiar songs touch heartstrings and can get your guests in a loving, rejoiceful frame of mind. If faith is an important aspect of your ceremony, musical selections that exemplify your religion can set a very nice, celebratory tone. If your budget allows, research local musicians who can provide live instrumental selections such as piano, harp, violin, cello, or guitar. At our wedding, my DJ happened to be a pianist as well, so we had the bonus of a live keyboard at our ceremony prelude and cocktail hour. That was a real treat. If you cannot opt for live music during the ceremony, recorded music to set the right tone is readily available.

Seating of the Family and Processional

Seating the family should happen just before the procession of the wedding party. Ideally, the groomsmen will cycle through, escorting all family members to their reserved seats, as the best man or closest bridal party member attends to the groom. Though traditionally escorted by her father or a father figure in her life, the bride may now be escorted by both parents or some combination of blended family members. Do what works best for you and your family and don't feel glued to old traditions. It's your day—make it work for you!

Nontraditional marriages offer a unique opportunity to be creative in how the marrying couple initially greets one another. I have seen traditional models here, with one member of the couple standing up front and being joined when the other member of the couple walks down the aisle. I have also seen couples walk down the aisle together. I enjoyed watching one couple be escorted individually down the aisle by their family until they joined each other. The ceremony can be as unique as your love, so here, again, do what feels right to you as a couple.

Mikhail Nilov

AMY'S FAVORITE TOUCHES

There are many wedding playlists available online. From those lists, choose songs for your own playlist and share it with your DJ to ensure your ceremony, prelude through recessional, sounds exactly as you wish.

Readings

Readings can hold a special place in the ceremony. Do you love poetry? Then include a love poem that touches you and exemplifies your love. Are you religious? Then include some passages that speak to your traditions and evoke your

> ### Amy's Personal Wedding Journey
>
> We chose Pablo Neruda's "Love Sonnet 17" for our wedding. We had this read in both English and Spanish because Cesar is from Colombia, South America, and many of his family members do not speak English. It helped them feel included in the ceremony and to witness our love just as strongly as the other guests. It also helped to symbolize the coming together of our two cultures and languages. I also love Wendell Berry's poem "What We Need Is Here" because it reminds the listener to be in the moment.

spirituality. Open a bottle of wine and spend some time as a couple researching quotations or excerpts that speak to your souls or exemplify your love or the marriage you aspire to have.

Use readings to highlight special things about your relationship and to strengthen the theme. Asking close friends or relatives who are not in your wedding party to perform readings is a great way to involve them in your ceremony.

Declaration of Intent

Now it's time to say, "I do!" The declaration of intent is the legally binding part of the ceremony. This is when you and your partner verbally acknowledge that you have both come to the ceremony of your own free will and that you desire to enter into marriage. After you legally declare your intent, you will exchange vows.

AMY'S FAVORITE TOUCHES

I love it when couples invite married members of their audience to silently renew their own vows alongside the wedding couple during their ceremony.

The Exchange of Wedding Vows

Your wedding vows can as traditional or as unconventional and unique as you wish. You may choose to follow protocol and have the officiant lead you through your promises to each other. These will sound very familiar. Or, you may wish to write your own vows. Here, my recommendation is to not feel pressured to be too personal or to write the greatest words of all time. Find your inspiration in vows online and then craft them into your own pledge to each other. If writing your own vows, you may each choose to write separate vows, or, as Cesar and I did, you may choose to write them together so that our promises were the same to each other.

Wine Ceremony

Special formalities can also be performed during your ceremony to weave in your wine theme in a tangible, visual way. You may use wine during the ceremony, for instance, to epitomize your new life together in a wine blending ceremony. Your officiant may announce that to symbolize and celebrate the blending of your two lives into one, they will invite you to perform a wine ceremony during which you

Olya Kobruseva

Amy's Personal Wedding Journey

For our vows, Cesar and I found a quiet spot at the beach, brought a picnic and some wine, and spent an afternoon dreaming about our future marriage and writing down the commitments that were important to us.

might pour individual half-carafes of wine into a large carafe together to represent your two lives blending into one. You could then take turns pouring a glass for each and make a toast, such as, "Now our lives are one."

The officiant could then say something like this:

> *This wine ceremony represents your two individual lives, combined like two wines, into one life. The drinking of the combined wine signifies the commitment you now make to live your lives as one family, and that you will now drink from the cup of life together. Marriage achieves the blending of hearts and lives. But let there be spaces in your new life together, so that each of you may nurture the individual growth of the other. Now, your separate lives will become one life, your separate homes one home, your separate fortunes one fortune, your separate dreams one dream. May you remember this day of promises you have sealed with the drinking of this new wine.*

Wine ceremonies symbolize family unity. *Asad Photography*.

> ### Amy's Personal Wedding Journey
>
> I made simple vow books to hold our wedding vows, and our attendants carried these for us. Every year on our anniversary we pull out these special books and read our vows again, helping us to remember the promises we made to one another and to bring up emotions of our incredible and unending commitment.

Of course, this should be altered to your liking, but can be a lovely ceremony when well-executed. The special wine glasses chosen for this ritual can be used over and over again on anniversaries as a keepsake to remember and renew your promises to one another.

Blessing

I like to include a blessing, read by a friend, someone in the bridal party, a family member, or the officiant, toward the end of a ceremony that lists the hopes and dreams you have for your wedding. These can be serious, as in the following:

> *May your life together be blessed with prosperity and good health. May you always share open and honest communication between each other. May you respect each other's individual talents and gifts and give full support to each other's professional and personal pursuits. May you cherish the home and family you will create together. May all the years to come be filled with moments to celebrate and renew your love. May you steadfastly act as a witness to each other's lives. May your love be a lifelong source of excitement, contentment, affection, respect, and devotion for one another.*

They can also be lighthearted, and read by the couple themselves, as in "I hope you always make me coffee in the morning

Garone Photography

and continue to take all the blankets at night and never replace the toilet paper roll." Either way, these wishes for your marriage should encapsulate who you are and what you want your relationship to be.

Recessional

Once the officiant states the blessing and proclaims you married, your recessional may begin! You and your new spouse will walk down the aisle hand in hand, followed by your family and wedding party, then the remaining guests. Unless you have taken photos before the ceremony, which is much less common, you will probably now be whisked away to some special spots on the property for organized photos with family and the wedding party. During this time, your guests are ready to begin socializing and partying, so let's now turn our attention to creating an awesome kickoff to your reception with an impressive cocktail hour.

Amy's Personal Wedding Journey

I saved every flower Cesar ever gave me while we dated and dried the petals. We handed out little organza bags of these with a note instructing guests to use the petals instead of rice during our recessional to shower us in love.

◀ Scope out places at your venue in which you can take photos after (or before) your ceremony. *K. Lenox Photography*

Heather Donald Photography

CHAPTER EIGHT

Enjoying a Spectacular Cocktail Hour

Once you are officially married, it is time to raise a toast with your loved ones at a spectacular cocktail hour! There are several ways in which you may weave your wine theme into your cocktail hour. Above all, you want your guests to be comfortable and getting into the party mood. Setting that mood with appetizers and excellent cocktails will not only start your party off right but also set the tone for the reception party to follow.

First things first, you will probably be taking photos with your bridal party and close family members and friends when your guests enter the cocktail hour, so you want to be sure they are being treated like royalty in your absence, because you are, after all, the host.

Cocktail hours are typically hosted by the bride and groom—meaning you should expect to pay for everyone's bar tab during that time. But there are no rules, and if you cannot do so, or prefer not to for a variety of reasons, you have options!

You may wish to *only* host cocktail hour, and then once cocktail hour is complete, the bar will transition to a cash bar, during which time guests will pay for their own drinks. If you choose this model, it's nice to provide a complimentary white or red wine pour with dinner. A wine pour offered at dinner is a great way to minimize your budget while also being a gracious host.

Alternatively, you may wish to host the entire evening, picking up the total bar tab. In this case, you may wish to carefully limit the timeframe so guests do not overdrink.

Finally, you may wish to not pay for drinks at all. If this is necessary for your budget, I still think a cocktail or wine pass should be provided, and I'll explain why a bit later.

I like to care for guests by making sure there is fruit-infused water available for self-serve, especially if a ceremony took place outdoors in the heat or sun. Citrus infusions such as lemon, orange, and lime are natural choices and look beautiful in large pitchers or glass urns with spigots. It's also nice to offer some unexpected choices, such as watermelon mint, cucumber melon, or berry infusions. Your venue may have what you need on hand to provide this service or you can purchase some lovely glass urns with pour spouts just about anywhere. The bonus is you get to keep them and use them for parties later!

AMY'S FAVORITE TOUCHES

An extra nice touch is to have eight- or ten-ounce plastic tumblers printed with your new monogram, a wedding phrase, or your names. These come in all shapes, sizes, and colors.

A flavored water station is a thoughtful touch. *Ta Focando*

Another thing to consider is that, depending on the size of your wedding, guests could be looking at a long bar line for that first drink. Simply put, once the ceremony is completed, everyone usually jets straight to the bar, and even the best of wedding venues with the highest level of service will have trouble keeping up with that huge influx of guests all at once. People will get grumpy, and we don't want that! We need people festive and hydrated. To avoid this problem, ensure that wait staff serve a complimentary signature cocktail or wine from trays. You may even wish to make these half-sized pours—such as three ounces of wine—or mini cocktails if budget is of concern. This small kindness makes the cocktail hour run more smoothly and keeps guests smiling!

Passed cocktails can prevent long lines at the bar right after the ceremony.
Shutterstock

Signature Cocktails

Now, to the fun part: creating a signature drink. Signature drinks are a favorite way of mine to really put your stamp on cocktail hour. You can create one cocktail that represents both of you or one to represent the bride and one to represent the groom. I've seen both ideas work really well! Of course, if the wedding is wine-themed, each cocktail recipe could include wine as a main or accenting ingredient.

Some couples get inspiration from their honeymoon destinations. For example, one couple created a tropical rum punch with cocktail umbrellas as their signature drink because they were going to Tahiti to celebrate their honeymoon. If choosing something meaningful like this, please be sure to include an explanatory sign at the bar to help guests make the connection. It's always a good idea to have cocktail hour signage, whether you have signature cocktails or not, to let guests know what is available and make ordering that much easier.

Cocktail hour signage helps guests know what is available and makes ordering easier. *Millyard Studios*

AMY'S FAVORITE TOUCHES

At one LaBelle Winery wedding, we served two drinks—one for the bride and one for the groom—that represented the parts of the country from which they came. The bride was from the South, so her drink was a Mint Julep. The groom was from New York, so his drink was a Manhattan.

I have had success creating signature cocktails that represent different heritages, relationship milestones, or simply something delicious the couple enjoys! For one couple, one bride liked beer and the other bride liked wine, so I created a summer shandy that incorporated both. Let the cocktail hour kick off your celebration with a personal touch.

Wine Cocktails

Since you may be creating a wine-themed wedding, may I entice you to include wine as a main ingredient in your signature cocktail? Wine cocktails are unique, interesting, slightly lower in alcohol, and downright delicious because they layer flavor on flavor. A nice touch would be to print copies of the recipe for guests so they can re-create your special cocktail at home and remember celebrating with you!

Let the following ideas and recipes inspire you!

THE HEMINGWAY

Ernest Hemingway, one of the greatest American authors, loved white rum and lime cocktails. During the halcyon days of summer 2012, my husband and I created this cocktail that makes delicious use of LaBelle Winery Seyval Blanc. Have a couple of these perfectly refreshing cocktails on a summer afternoon, and you won't care if it's ninety degrees outside!

- 3 ounces LaBelle Winery Seyval Blanc (or Sauvignon Blanc)
- 1 ounce white rum
- 1 ounce fresh grapefruit juice
- 1 ounce simple syrup or dash of agave nectar
- Splash of lime
- Fresh mint or lime wedge for garnish (optional)

Pour all ingredients into an ice-filled shaker and shake vigorously for at least 10 seconds. Either strain into a martini glass or pour over ice into a rocks glass. We like to add a sprig of fresh mint for garnish, but a lime wedge works just as well.

James Mojonnier

James Mojonnier

CRANBERRY WINE COSMOPOLITAN

Cesar and I often make this drink midweek for "date night" at home with a big bowl of popcorn—the perfect foil for this sweet, tart cocktail. It's also surprisingly good with pizza! It will delight your guests with its gorgeous pink color. Cranberry Wine Cosmopolitans can be made in large batches perfect for quick pouring at cocktail hour.

- 4 ounces LaBelle Winery Cranberry Wine
- 2 ounces triple sec (or Cointreau)
- 1 ounce fresh lime juice
- Colored sugar for rimming glasses
- Wedge of lime for garnish (optional)

Put all ingredients into an ice-filled shaker and shake vigorously for at least ten seconds. Pour into a sugar-rimmed martini glass and garnish with a lime wedge, if desired.

JALAPENO PEPPER WINE BLOODY MARY

Our brunch favorite is updated with our fiery Jalapeño Pepper Culinary Wine, which is made with 100% fermented jalapeño peppers. When combined with our house-made Bloody Mary Mix, there's no better way to begin brunch. I like to add a little extra horseradish for a bit more kick.

- 2 ounces LaBelle Winery Jalapeño Pepper Culinary Wine (or pepper vodka)
- 4 ounces good quality tomato juice
- 1 ounce fresh lime juice
- 1/2 teaspoon Worcestershire sauce
- 1/4 teaspoon horseradish
- 1/4 teaspoon salt
- 1/8 teaspoon pepper
- Choice of vegetable for garnish (optional)

Combine all liquid ingredients and pour into an ice-filled highball glass. Garnish with whatever you'd like! Celery is most common, but something unusual like green pepper slices, jicama, jalapeños, or asparagus stalks are fun too.

James Mojonnier

ENJOYING A SPECTACULAR COCKTAIL HOUR

James Mojonnier

THE GENTLEMAN'S MARTINI

My grandfather, whom we called "Boompa," rarely ever drank. Once in a great while, he would have an old-fashioned "high ball." What a great combination of flavors! It feels so manly and old Hollywood. But our version is not just for the boys. I wanted to update the old recipe with some fresh style and lighten it up. Here, LaBelle Winery Seyval Blanc shines, lifted substantially by fresh lemon and bitters. I love this cocktail before dinner.

- 2 ounces LaBelle Winery Seyval Blanc (or Sauvignon Blanc)
- 2 ounces good quality blended scotch
- 1 ounce fresh lemon juice
- 1/2 ounce simple syrup
- 1 1/2 ounce ginger ale
- Dash of bitters
- Twist of lemon for garnish

Place all liquid ingredients in an ice-filled shaker and shake vigorously. Strain into a new glass with fresh ice and enjoy with a twist.

SPRING EQUINOX

I woke up one morning with the recipe for this cocktail in my head! I went to the liquor store that day, searching for ingredients to bring my pear vanilla dream to reality. LaBelle Winery Riesling adds nice body to this recipe. The flavors of pears and vanilla perfectly complement each other, especially during the turn of seasons from winter to early spring. This cocktail is heavenly when served with a beautiful selection of artisan cheeses and crackers.

- 3 ounces LaBelle Winery (or other good quality semi-sweet) Riesling
- 2 ounces Grey Goose pear vodka (or your favorite pear vodka)
- 1/2 ounce vanilla simple syrup)
- Razor-thin slice of pear

Mix all ingredients but the pear slice in an ice-filled shaker and shake vigorously for 15 seconds. Strain into a martini glass and serve garnished with the pear slice.

VANILLA SIMPLE SYRUP:

Combine 2 cups water; 2 cups sugar; and a half a vanilla bean, split, in a small saucepan. Boil together until the sugar dissolves. Let the mixture simmer for 10 minutes, then cool and store it in a glass jar with the vanilla bean in the refrigerator for up to a month.

James Mojonnier

James Mojonnier

APRICOT SIESTA

My husband loves apricot brandy, so I created a cocktail around it featuring our very tropical Gewurztraminer. A sweet martini, this drink is fruit-forward, but balanced by the sparkling water and acid from the lemons or limes. This is an easy cocktail to batch ahead, making for a quick service at cocktail hour.

- 3 ounces LaBelle Winery (or other good quality) Gewurztraminer
- 1 ounce apricot brandy
- 1 ounce pineapple juice
- 1 ounce sparkling water
- 1 ounce apricot nectar
- Lime or lemon wedge and frozen grapes (optional) for garnish

Mix all liquid ingredients in an ice-filled shaker. Shake well and then strain into a martini glass. Squeeze lemon or lime wedge over the rim of the glass and float frozen grapes if desired. They are a great alternative to ice cubes!

SEYVAL BLANC MINT JULEP

We created the Seyval Blanc Mint Julep in honor of a Kentucky Derby party we held at LaBelle Winery. Customers and employees alike came bedecked in wide-brimmed hats, and we all felt just like southern belles sipping our juleps on a beautiful, sunshine-filled day. This julep is a bit lighter than the original, thanks to our Seyval Blanc. Adjust the sugar as you like it!

- 3 ounces LaBelle Winery Seyval Blanc (or Sauvignon Blanc)
- 1 1/2 ounces Kentucky bourbon (we prefer Woodford)
- 1/2 ounce simple syrup
- 2 lime wedges
- 10 mint leaves
- Additional fresh mint leaves for garnish

Muddle mint leaves in the bottom of a shaker, then place ice and remaining ingredients into the shaker and shake vigorously. Pour into an ice-filled highball glass (unless you have mint julep glasses!). Garnish with a sprig of mint.

James Mojonnier

James Mojonnier

BLUSH SANGRIA

The original version of this sangria was created for our Valentine's Day dinner at LaBelle Winery because it features our wine called Corazon, which means "heart" in Spanish. It's beautiful in a glass with the red fruit shining through. This version uses traditional sangria techniques, which originated in Spain hundreds of years ago. The result is as refreshing as it is beautiful.

- 24 ounces LaBelle Winery Corazon (or other good quality rosé)
- 6 ounces apple brandy
- 2 ounces peach or raspberry purée
- Assorted white or red fruit such as strawberries, apples, white grapes, and pears
- 1 ounce simple syrup or more to taste
- Club soda

A few hours before serving, place sliced fruit in a container such as a punch bowl or pitcher with brandy and 1 ounce of simple syrup (or two tablespoons of white sugar). A few hours before serving, add the fruit purée and bottle of wine to the container. When ready to serve, top off each ice-filled glass with an ounce of club soda. Garnish with the marinated fruit. This gorgeous blush sangria will delight your guests as a pre-dinner refresher. Enjoy!

SEYVAL BLANC MARGARITA

I love a classic margarita, but I've lightened this one up with the addition of our citrusy Seyval Blanc, and it is even better than the original! Create variations, such as a passionfruit margarita, by changing the juice added.

- 3 ounces LaBelle Winery Seyval Blanc (or Sauvignon Blanc)
- 1 ounce good quality tequila
- 1/2 ounce triple sec
- 1/2 ounce fresh squeezed lime juice
- 1/2 ounce simple syrup
- Slice of lime for garnish

Place ingredients into an ice-filled shaker and shake vigorously. Strain into a salt-rimmed highball glass for an "up" presentation, or serve on the rocks, and garnish with a lime slice.

James Mojonnier

James Mojonnier

SUMMER WHITE SANGRIA

Developed during my first season making wine with apples from Alyson's Orchard in Walpole, New Hampshire, and crafted with our flagship Dry Apple Wine, this white sangria is bright, citrusy, and cheerful! Use a clear glass pitcher so the beauty of the fruit shows through. Make double what you think you will need, because this sangria does not last! This is very popular at the winery, but it's so easy to make at home. It's an excellent drink for a cocktail hour because it can be prepared in advance.

- 24 ounces LaBelle Winery Dry Apple Wine (or good quality Pinot Grigio)
- 6 ounces apricot brandy (or, if none available, traditional brandy)
- 1 peach, sliced
- 1 apple, sliced
- 1 cup white grapes, sliced in half
- 1 lemon, sliced
- 1 lime, sliced
- 5 ounces simple syrup
- 4 ounces quality orange juice
- Club soda

Place fruit and brandy in a pitcher along with simple syrup and orange juice to marinate for at least three hours or overnight. Pour Dry Apple Wine into the pitcher and top with club soda just before serving. Serve over ice and garnish with marinated fruit.

WINEMAKER'S PINA COLADA

LaBelle Winery Gewurztraminer shines with pineapple and tropical notes, making it a natural fit for a summery drink inspired by the classic pina colada. Over ice, this drink begins many great evenings at the pool with my family. This would make a sweet reception cocktail for a couple headed for a tropical honeymoon.

- 1 1/2 ounces LaBelle Winery (or other good quality) Gewurztraminer
- 1 1/2 ounces coconut rum
- 3 ounces pineapple juice
- Fresh pineapple for garnish (optional)

Pour liquid ingredients into an ice-filled shaker and shake vigorously. Pour into an ice-filled highball glass and garnish with a slice of pineapple if desired.

James Mojonnier

WINEMAKER'S SMASH

A huge hit at LaBelle Winery, this drink is vacation in a glass! A classic rum punch, brightened by the sharp acidity of our Cranberry Wine, this drink will make you feel like you are lying on the beach in the Caribbean. The Winemaker's Smash is great for a reception because it can be made in batches.

- 2 ounces LaBelle Winery Cranberry Wine
- 1 1/2 ounce Brugal anejo rum (or your favorite anejo rum)
- 1 ounce good quality orange juice
- 1 ounce pineapple juice
- 1/2 ounce fresh lime juice
- 1/2 ounce simple syrup
- Splash of grenadine
- Orange and lime slices for garnish (optional)

Place ingredients into an ice-filled shaker and shake vigorously. Pour into a tall, ice-filled glass and garnish with orange and lime slices, if desired.

James Mojonnier

RASPBERRY WINE DAIQUIRI

A non-frozen take on the classic daiquiri popular in the 1980s, this sweet martini is saved from being cloying by the addition of lime juice.

- 3 ounces LaBelle Winery Red Raspberry Wine
- 1 1/2 ounces Bacardi white rum (or your favorite white rum)
- 1/2 ounce fresh squeezed lime juice
- 1/2 ounce simple syrup
- Fresh mint or a twist of lime for garnish)

Pour all ingredients into an ice-filled shaker and shake vigorously. Strain into a martini glass for an "up" presentation, or serve on the rocks. Garnish with either mint or a twist of lime. Frozen raspberries also make a nice garnish. Enjoy!

James Mojonnier

James Mojonnier

SUMMER SHANDY

A traditional shandy is half beer, half lemonade. We added LaBelle Winery Seyval Blanc in place of the lemonade and discovered a very uplifting summer treat! This cocktail satisfies both the wine and beer drinker, and it's a perfect cocktail to offer if one spouse enjoys wine and the other enjoys beer. This one can represent you both!

- 4 ounces LaBelle Winery Seyval Blanc (or Pinot Grigio)
- 4 ounces Samuel Adams Summer Ale (or other summer beer)
- 1/2 ounce lemon simple syrup
- Slice of lemon for garnish)

Pour chilled ingredients into a pilsner glass and garnish with a slice of lemon.

RIESLING BASIL MOJITO

Traditional mojitos are a Latin American bar staple. Our version is an easy-to-drink summer delight, and at LaBelle Winery, we make them with herbs picked fresh from our cedar garden boxes, which also provide us with fresh lettuces, tomatoes, peppers, and edible flowers used to prepare our bistro menu. Don't overdo the muddling in this recipe, or your drink will end up green—albeit a pretty shade of green.

- 2 ounces LaBelle Winery (or other good quality semi-sweet) Riesling
- 2 ounces white rum (or your favorite white rum)
- 5 basil leaves
- 5 mint leaves
- 1/2 ounce agave nectar
- 1/2 ounce fresh lime juice
- Basil or mint leaves or lime slices for garnish

Muddle the basil and mint together in the bottom of a shaker to release the oils. Add ice and all other ingredients and shake vigorously. Strain into an ice-filled highball glass and garnish with a fresh lime slice or sprig of basil or mint. Enjoy!

James Mojonnier

James Mojonnier

AUTUMN SHANDY

In 2012, when the season was changing from summer to autumn, I wanted to experiment with other versions of the shandy, which is typically a very summery drink traditionally made with beer and lemonade. A natural autumn choice was LaBelle Winery flagship Dry Apple Wine, to which we added our local favorite Samuel Adams Oktoberfest. The result is a layered and truly interesting autumn beer cocktail, perfect for sipping on those first chilly days of fall. Serve with a cinnamon sugar rim (optional).

- 4 ounces LaBelle Winery Dry Apple Wine (or Chenin Blanc), chilled
- 4 ounces Samuel Adams Oktoberfest (or other autumn or amber beer)
- Dash simple syrup
- Dash pure vanilla extract (we use LaBelle Winery Pure Vanilla Extract)

Pour chilled ingredients into a chilled pilsner glass and mix with a spoon. Enjoy!

MULLED APPLE WINE

Mulling wine dates back centuries to the Romans, where it is thought that they heated and flavored their wine to prevent it from spoiling. Charles Dickens solidifies mulled wine's place in literary and culinary history when he writes of mulled wine—typically made with dry red wine—in his classic *A Christmas Carol*. We've turned that recipe inside out, opting to use our Dry Apple Wine for a mulled wine spin on hot cider. It's a memorable delight showing the flavors of the season.

- 24 ounces LaBelle Dry Apple Wine (or light red wine)
- 1 1/2 cups water
- 1/2 cup brown sugar
- 4 cinnamon sticks
- 4 whole cloves
- 1/2 teaspoon ground nutmeg
- 1/2 orange, thinly sliced
- Additional cinnamon sticks for garnish

Combine water, sugar, and spices in a saucepan and bring to a boil. Boil for 5 minutes. Add orange slices, remove pan from the heat, and let sit for 15 minutes. Stir in the wine. Reheat gently over low heat, but don't allow it to boil. Serve very warm, in heated glasses or mugs, with a cinnamon stick as garnish. Makes 6 cups.

James Mojonnier

Cocktail Hour Wine

In your mind's eye, can you picture your guests being greeted by smiling servers holding trays of three-ounce wine pours? This makes for a lovely beginning to a phenomenal celebration. Not only will a wine pass at cocktail hour alleviate bar lines and get everyone in the party mood quickly but it will allow you to select wines that express your theme.

If you choose to offer only wine at your cocktail hour rather than a signature drink, there are a few guidelines you should follow. Wine before food needs to be carefully selected. Though your guests will undoubtedly be enjoying passed appetizers or stationary displays of treats during cocktail hour, their bellies and palates will not be ready for heavy wine.

For pre-dinner wine, it's best to keep it simple and light. That means sparkling wine, un-oaked white wines, or lighter red wines that are not heavy with tannins. Let's take a closer look.

Sparkling Wine

In the world of sparkling wine, you can hardly go wrong! Sparkling wine is a wide category made up of all things bubbly. This includes the best of the best, including the French sparkling wine known throughout the world as champagne, the Cadillac of sparkling wine.

Mèthode champenoise is a fermentation process that includes a secondary fermentation to produce the tiny bubbles we all love! This process is aided by hand-turning the bottles every week and otherwise leaving them undisturbed for over a year. The most prized champagnes in the world can be incredibly expensive because of the labor and process each bottle requires.

If your budget is unlimited, go for champagne! A wonderful kickoff to cocktail hour would be to greet

Champagne flutes are a must for celebrations and help the champagne hold its bubbles! *James Mojonnier*

guests with champagne on trays in tall flutes. But you do not have to break the bank for excellent sparkling wine.

Sparkling wines are made all over the world, not just in France. And typically, these other sparkling wines are more affordable. Take, for example, prosecco, an Italian sparkling wine that is brilliant and delightful and offered in a range of prices. It is an excellent alternative to champagne and especially good if being mixed with something else, as in a mimosa for a wedding brunch.

Prosecco is typically made from a different white grape variety than champagne, and that's okay! There are hundreds of awesome wine grape varieties and each offers something unique and special. It would be a shame to go through life drinking only chardonnay and wines made from chardonnay grapes when there are so many others to explore.

Another option is cava, a Spanish sparkling wine. Cava tends to be very affordable and definitely one of my go-to sparkling wines. I particularly love rosé cava, which is made from red grapes. Greeting guests with a pink cava will whet their appetites for the dinner celebration to come.

White Wine

When considering what white wine to pour prior to dinner, I like to think about the texture and mouthfeel of the wine and the predominant flavors presented. When consuming wine on its own or prior to an entrée, choose a wine that's not too heavy or

Amy's Personal Wedding Journey

We served prosecco, peach, and cranberry mimosas at our wedding brunch and they were a hit!

Mimosas are delightful at a brunch reception.
James Mojonnier

Passes of wine can also be served at cocktail hour.
Annika Wischnewsky

overburdened with oak. Your palate is simply not ready to receive it. Oak adds tannin to wine, and tannins dry out your mouth, so serving heavily tannic wines prior to dinner is a no-no.

For cocktail hour, I like to stick with acidic white wine that has not been aged in oak. Wines that are fragrant, such as Sauvignon Blanc or Seyval Blanc, can really do the trick here, delighting the palate and nose in preparation for the meal to come. A Chenin Blanc, Pinot Grigio, or Pinot Gris will also fit the bill nicely for this timeframe. Be sure to ask your venue to not *over-chill* your white wine, which should be served between 45 and 50 degrees. Considering most refrigeration keeps contents below 40 degrees, the wine will need a bit of time to warm up prior to serving. Serving white wine too cold dulls its flavors and impedes your ability to perceive the most beautiful nuances of the wine. If you go through the trouble of hand-selecting a wine, you want it served at its peak.

Red Wine

Offering red wine before dinner can be tricky, but it can be done! Simply select red wines that are not heavy in tannins or too oaky, just as you would white wines. Opt for fruit-forward, jammy varieties with zippy acidity to get that palate ready for dinner. Consider Pinot Noir, with its lighter tannin and typical cherry undertones, or a zinfandel that has not been aged too long in oak. Blended red wines are also a great bargain and flavor profile for cocktail hour. And, there are Cabernet Sauvignons and Syrahs that won't overwhelm a pre-dinner palate. A bottled sangria might be a festive beginning as well. The key here is to taste these reds prior to selecting them for your wedding. I know! I know! Such hard work! But wines vary so much by the winemaker that you'll never really know until you try them. Or consult a wine expert or wine store owner to guide you toward fruity, no-food-required reds. Your guests will thank you.

Cocktail Hour Appetizers

Your cocktail hour is a time to really impress your guests with delicious appetizers and beverages that complement them. Your guests are likely hungry, thirsty, and ready to mingle. Treat them with a symphony of flavors to delight their palates and prepare them for the celebration feast to come.

Passed Appetizers

Server-passed appetizers are a lovely way to greet guests and a great opportunity to reinforce your wine theme. Let's begin with the platters upon which these

AMY'S FAVORITE TOUCHES

I consider different dietary needs, tastes, and guest preferences when selecting four to five passed appetizers that offer a spectrum of gluten-free, vegetarian, and keto-friendly selections in addition to traditional choices. You can't please everyone, but variety is key.

bite-sized treats can be served. No doubt, your venue already owns vessels used to serve appetizers, but you should ask to review these, because you may wish to supply your own.

One option would be simple wooden planks (make sure they are food-grade) that are the color of wine barrels. If you use these, it's also complementary to use a galvanized mini bucket for any sauces or dips.

Guests enjoy cocktail hour.
K. Lenox Photography

Antique metal trays often found at flea markets or antiques shows are another option. I also love large slate boards for this purpose, as they are rustic but elegant and show off food beautifully. Especially nice are wooden trays made from upcycled wine barrels. Just make sure they are not too large because they can get heavy for the servers once loaded with food.

Working with your venue and the executive chefs, you should be able to customize your menu to play up your wine theme. You may wish to consider passed appetizers with wine reduction sauces or wine-infused dips.

The following are some wine-infused ideas for your passed appetizers.

Stationary Hors D'oeuvres

While your guests are enjoying mixing, mingling, and munching on passed appetizers, I suggest offering a stationary option—that is, a large plated display of delicious treats—in addition to passed appetizers.

Large cheese and charcuterie displays are an obvious and excellent choice. Not only do cheese and cured meats go perfectly with wine, they also can be displayed beautifully. I like cheese displays that offer five critical elements: height, cheese variety, color, texture, and something fresh. To accomplish this, you'll need a willing chef who understands the artistic appeal of a great cheese and charcuterie presentation.

For height, use varying display pieces to elevate certain items. Upturned bowls, tiered cake stands, and the like work well. Height may also come from your chosen foods. For example, tall cheese or breadsticks can be shown on end in a cylindrical container such as a vase or glass. Cheese variety should be created by offering cheese from different

A gorgeous cheese display is always a hit at cocktail hour.
Ashley Olafsson

milk sources. I like to offer one cow, one goat, and one sheep's milk cheese for variety, as each offers a different flavor profile. Mark each with cheese markers, which you can find online or make yourself!

Color is critical in eye-pleasing displays. Ask the chef to provide every color of the rainbow with a blue or purple jam selection, a grainy mustard, bright white dips, a green fresh element such as grapes, some pops of red with radish flowers, different color chips such as beet chips and breads for dipping, and other items that bring life and color to your station. Be sure to include some gluten-free crackers. Different textures should also be provided: soft and hard cheeses, crunchy chips, supple breads, sharp mustards, and crisp vegetables. Fresh elements such as juicy grapes cascading from a high-tiered plate, should always be included to off-set the display of cured meats and cheeses. For fresh vegetables, I like unexpected items such as jicama or blanched asparagus spears.

With this kind of attention to your selections, your cheese and charcuterie display will stand out and please every one of your guests.

Mediterranean displays are also greatly enjoyed by guests! Consisting of bowls of hummus; whipped feta cheese; olives; soft pita bread; tabbouleh; baba ghanoush; roasted vegetables in balsamic and olive oil; and grilled, skewered meats, these selections are very well complemented by wine of all kinds and will delight your loved ones. Many of these dishes can be made with wine as an ingredient to further weave your wine theme into the menu.

Brunch weddings can showcase a spectacular carved fruit station with artfully cut watermelons, cantaloupes, honeydews, pineapple, berries, and kiwi. On these types of displays, I love to include mini martini glasses filled with "drunken berries," which are blackberries, blueberries, and raspberries tossed in a sweet wine and topped with wine-infused whipped cream and garnished with mint. Place tiny spoons aside them for guests to dig in.

Now you know how to lavish guests with a fun, unique, and wine-infused cocktail hour filled with treats to delight all the senses. Implementing even a few of these suggestions creates excitement for the celebration to come! How will you top this amazing cocktail hour? With a reception that weaves wine into your décor and menu in a stunning way.

CHAPTER NINE

Celebrating in (Wine) Style

Your moment has arrived after months (maybe years) of planning. Now is the time to reap what you have sown! Let's take a look at how you can crush the details for your wine-themed wedding reception with style and in a way that allows you to really bask in the moment as a couple.

Your guests will remember loads of details and have wonderful memories of your wedding celebration, but what will they talk most about? The food! It is *all about the food*. Create a memorable menu with small touches that take it from ordinary to extraordinary.

Your wine-themed wedding menu should showcase wine as a main or accenting ingredient to really weave in your concept. Why? Because creating excellent food is an artistry that requires layering flavors, and wine is an ingredient that can take our taste buds to a whole other level. With the right planning, you can also ensure that your menu choices perfectly pair with your dinner wine choices.

First things first, let's talk about timing. Timing your reception properly is so important, and to do this, you must think about your priorities. Adhering to

AMY'S *LEAST* FAVORITE TOUCH

I recently saw a wedding party enter with shots in their hands and then they all did the shots on the dance floor together. My advice? Don't do this. You don't actually want people drunk at your wedding. Keep things simple and classy.

longstanding but time-sucking traditions, such as garter ceremonies (I have not seen one of these in years) or receiving lines, will take time away from eating and dancing. Is a five-course meal important to you? If so, that's great! But it'll cost you time on the dance floor.

Consider these elements and how much time you'll devote to each:

- Receiving line after ceremony
- Photos
- Bridal party arrivals and introductions
- Toasts
- Dinner
- First dance
- Guest dancing
- Bouquet and garter toss
- Cake cutting
- Late night snacks
- Final farewell

Your reception is just that: yours. Do not feel obligated to do any or all of the traditions, and feel free to make up new traditions. Make your own traditions and keep it authentic to you as a couple and you can't go wrong.

Menu Planning and Timing

Once you have thought through how much focus you would like put on the food and meal courses, you can begin to make decisions that shape your menu. You'll need to decide whether you'd prefer a cocktail-style reception with stations of food that guests may visit as they are mingling and dancing, or whether you prefer a more formal, sit-down meal.

Cocktail Reception and Stations-Style Reception

I love a well-executed cocktail reception-style event because it never feels too formal or stuffy and allows guests the freedom to mingle with other guests not seated at their table. For this type of reception to work well, you need to consider the variety of food stations so lines don't form, and provide sufficient options so guests can make a full meal out of the choices. Dotting stations around the room is a great way to keep the crowd moving and flowing, although having an assigned seat for everyone is still recommended.

Cocktail hours should have at least two appetizer stations in addition to a choice of three passed appetizers, two protein stations, a salad station, and starch options, such as pastas or baked potatoes, added.

Stationary hors d'oeuvres are a must in a cocktail-style reception. Typically, I suggest cheese and charcuterie displays (with accompaniments such as grainy mustards and dried and fresh fruits such as figs, pickled vegetables, and jam), Mediterranean tapas (complete with olive tapenade,

Amy's Personal Wedding Journey

For my wedding, I chose to skip the bouquet toss and, instead, spoke a few heartfelt words (in Spanish!) to my new mother-in-law, who only speaks Spanish, as I handed her the bouquet. It was a beautiful moment that I cherish. You can never earn enough brownie points with your mother-in-law!

Dachowski Photography

Anna Stabile

bruschetta, hummus, spiced feta dip, baba ghanoush, and plenty of pita and crackers), fresh fruit displays (perfect for brunch weddings served with minted yogurt, honey, and granola), and, of course, the classic vegetable crudité (built with roasted as well as fresh, crunchy vegetables and a killer dip). Chefs can prepare each of these recipes to have wine in them to further your wine theme.

Passed hors d'oeuvres should be chosen to complement what you are offering at the stations. For example, don't choose a cheese-based passed appetizer if you are already offering a cheese display. You want variety. Also be sure to consider various dietary needs when making your choices so everyone feels included. It's considerate to have at least one vegetarian and one keto/gluten-free appetizer if you can do so. Take a look at this list for some ideas for passed appetizers that can be made with wine and all of which we have served successfully at LaBelle Winery.

- Tomato Confit Bruschetta
- Pesto Parmesan Arancini
- Spinach and Feta Stuffed Mushrooms
- Spicy Sausage and Cheddar Stuffed Mushrooms
- Crispy Mac and Cheese Bites
- Fried Plantain Chip, Cilantro, Tomato and Smokey Lime Crema
- Buffalo Cauliflower Bite with Blue Cheese Fondue
- Pork Pot Stickers with Ponzu
- White Wine-Poached Shrimp Cocktail with Jalapeno Pepper Wine Cocktail Sauce
- Wine-Brined Curried Chicken Salad with Coconut Phyllo
- Wine-Brined Buttermilk Fried Chicken Bite with Spicy Honey
- Bacon-Wrapped Sea Scallops

- Red Wine-Marinated Mediterranean Beef Skewers
- Red Wine-Marinated Beef Tenderloin Skewers with Wine Steak Sauce
- Mini Lobster Salad Tacos with White Wine Aioli
- Coconut Shrimp in Riesling Chili Sauce
- Smoked Salmon Mousse with White Wine on Cucumber Rounds
- Wagyu Meatballs with Riesling Sweet and Sour Sauce

Anna Stabile

AMY'S FAVORITE TOUCHES

At one LaBelle wedding, we featured a raw bar with a rainbow of caviar types, a giant cornucopia spilling cocktail shrimp onto a hand-carved ice table, as well as king crab legs and oysters, shucked to order. Of course, I was happy to create a wine-based mignonette sauce to accompany the oysters.

Buttermilk Chicken Bites with Hot Honey. *James Mojonnier*

Mac and cheese bites. *James Mojonnier*

Stuffed mushrooms. *James Mojonnier*

In addition to these appetizers, your stations will need to include a culinary station or two. Think along the lines of a pasta station at which pasta is cooked in various sauces, a taco bar, or a raw bar with all the trimmings. Raw bars are always incredibly impressive. They can be taken to extremes if the budget allows.

For protein-based carving stations, opt for wine barrel smoked tenderloin of beef with house-made bearnaise made with wine reduction, peppercorn crusted beef sirloin with horseradish cream, slow-roasted prime rib au jJus, or roast turkey with spiced cranberry jam and a wine demi-glace.

A brunch wedding lends itself so well to the cocktail reception style. *James Mojonnier*

Beef skewers. *James Mojonnier*

Fig and prosciutto. *James Mojonnier*

Caprese skewers. *James Mojonnier*

> ### *Amy's Personal Wedding Journey*
>
> Cesar and I styled a station party so guests could mingle and graze as our two families blended into one. Our menu? Apricot-Glazed Ham carving station with roasted baby potatoes, Wood-Fired Tenderloin with Horseradish Cream, a fruit display with brûlée grapefruit, and a pastry station with my husband's favorite: French croissants. In addition, we offered mini pancake stacks on skewers, scallops wrapped in prosciutto, a cheese display, and, for dessert, a chocolate fountain. We also offered a mimosa bar with various fruits and juices. This style allowed us to begin celebrating right away. For us, it was perfect.

Formal Seated, Plated Meal

If you choose to have a sit-down meal, I recommend three courses plus a dessert buffet. The timing of these courses is critical to the success of your event and getting your guests up on their feet and dancing.

The first course can easily be an *amuse bouche,* which literally means "an amusement of the mouth" in French! An amuse bouche needs to be spectacularly pretty and should be dropped in place a few moments before cocktail hour ends and guests are invited to take their seats. I like an amuse bouche that is artistic and can be consumed in one bite, perhaps served in a decorative spoon or a small skewer or bamboo serving piece. To go with your wine theme, consider having the amuse bouche also contain wine as an ingredient.

Which small bite to serve? One approach is to serve something to take the place of a full course. For example, if you don't want to serve a soup course, you could serve a mini soup shooter as an amuse bouche. Or, instead of a salad course, you could serve a mini composed salad as an amuse bouche. For inspiration, consider the ideas on the next page.

- An Oyster with Wine Mignonette
- Riesling Goat Cheese with Herbs
- Gougeres with Wine Compound Butter
- Radish Slices with Compound Wine Butter with Sea Salt Flakes
- Deviled Egg with Wine Aioli
- Crab Salad Toast Point with Wine Reduction
- Timbale of Shaved Beef Carpaccio with Red Wine Reduction
- Seyval Blanc Ceviche of Scallop
- Mini Caprese Salad on a Skewer with Red Wine Balsamic Glaze
- Mini Watermelon Feta Salad with Basil and Mint
- Salmon Mousse with Chardonnay Drizzle on Cucumber
- Single Veggie Sushi with Wasabi Rice Wine Aioli
- Mini Lobster Roll on Brazilian Pan de Queso with Seyval Blanc Aioli Dressing
- Avocado Mousse on a Plantain Chip with Pico de Gallo Garnish and Lime
- Mini Cheese and Charcuterie Course with a Flourish of Wine Jam and Grainy Mustard

Once your guests are seated and introductions and toasts have been made, it is time for the first course. To compress time, think about whether you would mind servers dropping the first course during speeches and toasts. You may not want the distraction, but it will make dinner fly and get you on the dance floor faster.

Amy's Personal Wedding Journey
Cesar and I provided coloring books and crayons for children who attended our wedding to keep them busy and happy.

Salad Course

I love a salad course before dinner in the warmer months, mostly because it is an opportunity to incorporate wine in a zingy, delicious wine vinaigrette that gets your palate ready for a phenomenal dinner.

Composed salads are my favorite. A composed salad is a salad with structure, such as a cucumber wrapped salad, that has height and is unique from salads you would make yourself at home. I also love to present salads with special ingredients, such as edible flowers and herbal garnishes, that are unusual and delight your invitees. I once planned a wedding with a trio of salads on one long plate—each with its own personality—to rave reviews!

Soup Course

In the cooler months it is comforting to present a soup course in place of salad, and here I let the seasons guide me. Autumn soups, such as butternut apple bisque made with Dry Apple Wine or Riesling and garnished with pumpkin seeds, are incredible. What's more, this soup can be made vegetarian, dairy-free, and gluten-free to satisfy all your guests' dietary needs.

Lobster bisque is always a great option and, when made right, is undeniably delectable. It is also a treat for your guests because it is a soup rarely made at home due to the complexity of the recipe. Top with a flourish of coconut cream and lemongrass and double check that the recipe uses wine, which is typically sherry.

Main Course

Your main course really needs to shine at your wedding celebration. Incorporating your wine theme into your main course will make pairing wine with your meal a snap.

Offering your guests a choice of entrées

Photos by James Mojonnier

James Mojonnier

is always desirable. If your budget allows, a duet plate—that is, a plate with two protein choices in one—is a great solution to the age-old problem of pleasing everyone. A duet of surf and turf, for example, could include lobster and beef, or chicken and salmon, or a filet of beef Oscar, which is a filet topped with crab meat. I have also seen beautiful presentations of braised short ribs and scallops, ord chicken and shrimp. Of course, a vegetarian option should be offered as well.

All these choices can be prepared with wine in mind! The following selections are a good start toward featuring wine in your wedding menu:

- Red Wine-Marinated Filet Mignon with Caramelized Onions and Bearnaise Sauce
- Grilled Ribeye with Wine-Infused Compound Butter

- Red Wine-Braised Short Ribs with Mushrooms and Pearl Onions
- White Wine-Roasted Filet of Haddock with Lemon Basil Crumb and Wine Cream Sauce
- Wine-Roasted Atlantic Salmon with Olive and Herb Salad
- Wine-Brined Pork Loin with Roasted Apples and Pancetta Bacon Crumble
- Stuffed Chicken Saltimbocca with Alpine Cheese, Sage, Prosciutto, and Red Wine Reduction
- Herb-Roasted Statler Breast of Chicken with Seyval Blanc Wine Cream Sauce

James Mojonnier

Heather Donald Photography

- Za'atar-Dusted Cauliflower Steak, Roasted Peppers, Grilled Broccolini, and Red Wine Hummus
- Mediterranean Eggplant Tower with Herbed Ricotta and Artichokes with Red Wine Balsamic Reduction

And for duet plates, we recommend:

- Slow Roasted Wine-Braised Sirloin with Crab Stuffed Jumbo Shrimp in Red Wine Demi Glace and a Beurre Blanc Sauce
- Petite Filet Mignon and Butter Poached Lobster Tail with Red Wine Demi Glace
- Herb Roasted Petite Chicken Breast and Atlantic Salmon in a White Wine Velouté with Tomato Caper Relish

Dessert Displays

Whether you offer a cocktail reception; brunch wedding reception; or traditional, sit-down dinner, I feel that dessert should be placed buffet style after the dancing begins. Anything else confines guests to their seats for too long, and really steals time away from celebrating on the dance floor.

You will likely have slices of your wedding cake prepared on plates for guests to choose off the buffet. To supplement these, couples offer myriad confections to enjoy as well. A Viennese display of tiny desserts is a great choice, as is a good old-fashioned cookies and milk display with fun straws, chocolate milk in mini glass milk jugs, whipped cream, and chocolate

Dessert buffets make for a sweet ending. *K. Lenox Photography* ➤

Late-night snacks are a great send-off. *LaBelle Winery*

shavings. A coffee station is another smart idea near the dessert buffet. Ask your venue if they can arrange an espresso and cappuccino station, if your budget allows, as a special treat. You may need to source an outside vendor for this indulgence, but it will be worth it.

Some other ideas for dessert displays are mini presentations of chocolate mousse, mini cake, mini crème brûlée, or an Italian cookie display. These must be meticulous and gorgeous, garnished with fresh berries, spun sugar, and brûléed citrus fruits or edible flowers.

Late Night Snacks

After all that drinking and dancing, it is wonderful to offer a fresh buffet of late-night snacks to your guests before they hit the road.

Late night snacks should be fun and imaginative. My favorite is to offer giant German-style pretzels with various wine-infused mustards and butters. These offerings should throw health to the wind and just be plain amusing. It's a pleasurable way to send your guests off with full bellies and warm hearts.

Some other ideas could be:

- Mini taco bar with all the fixings
- Beef or fried chicken sliders with accompaniments and french fries served in cones
- Assorted mini flatbreads and pizzas
- Breakfast sandwiches wrapped in wax paper and twine
- Nacho bar
- Ice cream bar
- Cookies and milk (chocolate, almond, and strawberry)

How to Select Wine for Your Reception

With all this effort placed on creating a flawless menu, you'll need to choose the perfect wines to complement the food. Wine selection is so important and can

Shutterstock

really enhance the taste of the food with which it is paired. This is no myth—wine really does enhance your food when chosen correctly.

The Toast Champagne

To select the perfect bubbly to use as your wedding toast wine, consider budget, personal taste, and timing. Typically, a venue will set out the sparkling wine during the cocktail hour when they are setting the tables, and, as such, the bubbly will sit for some time. Consider your event timing to ensure it sits for no longer than fifteen minutes or it will become room temperature and not so bubbly. That being the case, you may not wish to break the bank on this two-ounce pour. Most people do not even drink this whole glass of champagne during the toast, so I think it is better to pour a less expensive sparkling wine and save your money for other touches. Of course, you can opt for something special at your table if that is important to you. If your reception is at a winery, consider their sparkling wine, if they offer one.

AMY'S FAVORITE TOUCHES

I love when younger guests are included in the toasts with a ginger ale pour, with a cherry dropped into it (to clearly denote the non-alcoholic beverage). Then they can feel part of the fun and tradition!

The Dinner Wine

Your dinner wine selections will be driven by your entrée choices, even if you choose a cocktail-reception-style event. If offering carving stations or having a cocktail reception event, where guests will attend the stations of their choosing, base the wine choices offered at the bar on the two main protein stations. Offer one white and one red that are versatile. Stay away from heavily oaked wines such as Chardonnay and California Cabernet and opt for medium-body styles with a mid-level of tannin to complement a wide variety of food.

Also, even though your event revolves around mingling and stations, you could still add an air of formality with a wine pour at the table. Servers should offer the choice of a three- or four-ounce pour of red or white as selected.

A more formal menu requires the perfect pairing of wine, and that can be accomplished at your menu tasting prior to your event. If you are not confident

Heather Donald Photography

in selecting wine, bring along a friend or family member who is to assist, or ask the venue if they have an expert on staff. As a winemaker, picking the perfect wine pairing is something I'm very passionate about and, as such, I'm always happy to offer this service to our couples. It takes time and practice to be good at this.

Dinner wines should be elegant and crowd pleasing. That is to say, do not select wines that are "out there" in terms of huge flavors, tannins, and oak. For this reason, I prefer wine made in the old-world style or ones from Europe that seem to find a way to complement without overpowering the meal.

If your budget allows, a wine pour with dinner is a thoughtful touch, rather than only offering wine at the bar. This may be offered instead of an open bar if desired.

Plan also to offer dessert wines at your bar or poured directly at your dessert buffet. Dessert wines, such as port, are a sweet way to end the celebration.

All this meticulous planning will create for you and your guests a memorable, delicious, and fun-filled celebration to mark the beginning of your life's journey with your partner. You will bask in the glow and congratulate yourself on an event well planned as you embark on your new life together, filled with the memories of your friends and family celebrating the most precious gift of all—your love for one another!

CHAPTER TEN

Designing Wine-Themed Thank-You Notes

The celebrations are over, and you are now married! Hopefully you have had a chance to honeymoon and really get into your groove as a couple. You may even be getting used to saying, "my husband" or "my wife."

Many people have given their time, resources, and gifts to help make your wedding one of the best days of your life. Call me old-fashioned, but I believe a handwritten thank-you note is in order.

Current etiquette rules are such that it is generally considered acceptable if thank-you notes are sent within three or four months of the wedding, but I disagree. You should not let six weeks pass before you let those you love know how much you appreciate their involvement in your special day. In addition, should you receive gifts before the wedding, it's best to send out those thank-yous within two weeks of their receipt.

You have options for wine-themed wedding thank-yous that will remind guests of their awesome time celebrating with you.

Photo Cards

One approach is to select a favorite photograph from your wedding day and make note cards from that photo. This could be a large group photo of everyone in attendance, a beautiful photo of the ceremony, a joyous photo of the entire bridal party after the ceremony, or a romantic photo of just you as a couple. Some family members may frame this thank-you note as a keepsake, so keep that in mind when you choose your photo.

Many websites offering this printing service can produce these cards quickly. I do not recommend that you print your thank-you message in an impersonal manner inside the card. These messages should always be handwritten. However, I do find it lovely to print a photo on the front of a note card with your new married name (in our case, "Thank you from The Arboledas"). Inside, you could include a verse from one of your readings or from your vows to remind people of the sentiment of the day.

I would not break the bank on these types of notes as, let's face it, most people will throw them away. Do take the time, however, to design it well and complete your wedding celebration with class.

Thank-You Notes in the Invitation Design

Another option is to design your thank-you notes at the same time you design your invitations. In this way, you can create a stationary package that runs on the same theme and style for the entire affair. Your save-the-date announcements, official invitations, wedding programs, and thank-you notes can all share the same paper, color scheme, and theme.

This option works very well if your theme and design are memorable and unique. For example, if your stationary choice involves

Turn your wedding photos into thank-you notes and create special mementos for those who attended. *James Mojonnier*

AMY'S FAVORITE TOUCHES

Specialty boxes may be found and printed at various online sources.

Shutterstock

unique paper—let's say, kraft paper—with special marking appliques, ink choice, or ribbon or twine. Carrying that through all four possible paper productions is a nice touch.

A stationary package might also be more cost-effective because, as with all printing, the more you print at one time, the less each piece costs.

Specially Designed Thank-You Notes and Small Gifts

If your budget allows, it is absolutely spectacular to send a small token gift as part of a thank-you package, especially with the wine theme. The sky is the limit with regard to how fancy these can be.

For example, you could include corkscrews personalized with your names or your monogram and date, so that every time a guest opens a bottle of wine, they can remember the special memories they made at your wedding celebration. Another option is a custom wine stopper, otherwise called a bar top. These typically have a plastic or wooden decorative top attached to a cork bottom that may be inserted into a bottle to maintain its quality after opening.

Thank-You Wording

Below I suggest a bit of wording to get you going on your note writing. I like to vary notes from person to person and make them individual. Thank-you notes should not feel like you cut and pasted each note exactly the same for each guest. You invited specific people to your wedding, so the thank-you note should be specific to them, and you should take the time to personalize it for that guest.

Here's a sample thank-you for guests who purchased a gift from your wedding registry and attended the wedding.

> *Dear [guest name(s)],*
> *Thank you for joining us on our wedding day and thank you so much for your generous gift. We are so excited to use the [insert gift and be specific in how you will use it]. We'd love to have you over for drinks and dinner to showcase our [insert gift and what you can do with it]. Thank you for being a part of making such a special day happen.*
>
> *Warmly,*
> *[your names]*

Here's a sample thank-you for guests who gave you a money gift and attended the wedding.

> *Dear [guest name(s)],*
> *Thank you so much for being a part of our special day! We are so grateful for your generous gift. We will be putting it toward the [closing costs of our new home, saving for a new home together, etc.]. We can't wait to have you over for a visit once we're settled!*
>
> *All the best,*
> *[your names]*

Here's a sample thank-you for wedding guests who contributed to your honeymoon fund and attended the wedding.

> Dear [guest name(s)],
> Thank you so much for being there on our wedding day. We hope you had as much fun as we did! We are so thankful for your generous contribution to our honeymoon fund. We'll be putting it toward our special excursion to [insert destination here] later this year and we'll definitely send you a photo or a postcard! Thank you for helping us make lifelong memories.
>
> Hope to see you soon,
> [your names]

Here's a sample thank-you for guests who traveled to get to your wedding or attended your destination wedding.

> Dear [guest name(s)],
> We're so grateful you were able to make the trip to celebrate our wedding day with us. You made the day so special, and we hope you enjoyed the weekend away. We truly appreciate the time and resources used for this travel that allowed you to help us make memories that will last a lifetime.
>
> Love,
> [your names]

Millyard Studios

Here's a sample thank-you for people who didn't attend but sent a gift.

Dear [guest name(s)],
Thank you so much for the beautiful set of baking dishes. It was so nice of you to honor us and our marriage in this way! We wish you could have celebrated with us in person on our wedding day, but hopefully we can get together soon so we can share our memories and photos with you!
Sincerely,
[your names]

Here's a sample thank-you for wedding vendors.

Dear [vendor name(s)],
Thank you for the [awesome musical entertainment you provided on our wedding day]. Our guests couldn't stop talking about how amazing [your music] was! Thank you so much for bringing our vision to life and helping us make lifelong memories!

Sincerely,
[your names]

Here's a sample thank-you for your parents and close family.

Dear [guest name(s)],
Thank you so much for everything you did to make our big day happen. It wouldn't have been possible without you. Your love and support mean the world to us, and we're so excited for everything to come. We are so grateful we could make these lifelong memories with you.

All our love,
[your names]

Here's a sample thank-you for your bridesmaids.

Dear [bridesmaid's name],
Thank you so much for being with me on my big day, and for everything you did to help make our wedding happen. We couldn't have done it without you!
Love,
[your name(s)]

Here's a sample thank-you for people who weren't invited but sent a gift.

Dear [gift-giver name(s)],
Thank you so much for generously marking our wedding celebration with a gift! We are so appreciative of your kind gesture and look forward to showing you a photo or two upon our return from our wedding and honeymoon.
Sincerely,
[your names]

Even if you have to spend a little extra time on your thank-you notes, it will mean the world to those receiving them. A little appreciation goes a long way and will certainly brighten someone's day.

LaBelle Winery

Conclusion

I hope this book has helped you visualize that a wine-themed wedding will not only make your wedding easier to plan but also lend a feeling of timelessness and elegance to your celebration. A wine-themed wedding puts you squarely in the timeline of centuries of tradition and connects you with history, art, science, and that which binds us all—love.

Winemakers love their craft and make sacrifices for it, which makes wine a fitting metaphor for marriage indeed. Including your guests on this journey will elevate your celebration.

You have envisioned your dream wine wedding and considered all the details. Now it's time to execute your big plans for a celebration to remember. I hope the time you spend planning and anticipating your wedding will be filled with joy. Make choices authentic to you as a couple and let your creativity and imagination shine through! If you do this, you will feel comfortable as you celebrate a wedding that represents who you are. Please take my ideas and make them your own for a celebration that reflects you as a couple. But most of all, remember that love has brought you to this point and it is through love that you will most enjoy your wedding day.

I wish you lifelong love, the kind that still gives you butterflies even after decades, and I wish for you that you'll always hold your wedding day memories as the happiest moments of your life.

Wine-Themed Wedding Checklist

There are many exhaustive wedding checklists available. Here, I outline a checklist for a wine-themed wedding.

- ☐ Choose a venue
- ☐ Set a date
- ☐ Determine wine theme and color scheme
- ☐ Give thought to budget
- ☐ Map out guest list
- ☐ Create web page
- ☐ Choose wedding party
- ☐ Choose wedding party attire in a wine-themed color scheme and accessories
- ☐ Choose and book ceremony location
- ☐ Book caterer, if one is needed, and discuss wine-themed menus
- ☐ Book florist and determine how wine-themed elements may be incorporated
- ☐ Determine menu through tastings of wine-infused food and wine pairings
- ☐ Create wine-themed wedding cocktails
- ☐ Book your cake baker and discuss wine-themed cake ideas
- ☐ Design and create wine-themed save-the-date cards, invitations, and thank-you cards
- ☐ Create or purchase wine-themed favors and table décor
- ☐ Consider wine-themed place cards and table numbers
- ☐ Write vows
- ☐ Choose nature, vineyard, or wine-themed readings for ceremony
- ☐ Discuss unity ceremony including wine
- ☐ Order or begin to build wine-themed wedding welcome baskets for traveling guests
- ☐ Purchase wine-themed wedding party and parent gifts
- ☐ Create wine-themed favors for guests
- ☐ Choose final wine pairings

About the Author

Kristin Hardwick Photography

AMY LABELLE is the founder of and winemaker at LaBelle Winery. Formerly a corporate attorney practicing in Massachusetts and New Hampshire, her lifelong interest in wine led her to open LaBelle Winery to pursue her passion for winemaking. LaBelle Winery has developed into a destination winery, and Amy has slowly seen her dream realized: to focus on making world-class wine in New Hampshire and create exceptional food and wine experiences for her guests.

Amy lives in New Hampshire with her husband, Cesar Arboleda, and her two boys, Jackson Alejandro and Lucas Cesar. In her free time, Amy enjoys spending time with her family, especially watching her two sons excel at various sports. Amy also loves to nourish her family with meals cooked from scratch, enjoys entertaining her friends and family in her home, and reading. Amy's perfect day would be spent with her family on a beach anywhere with good food and wine and a ball to toss around with her boys.

Write to Amy at amy@labellewinery.com, and she just might share her secret recipes with you. Follow Amy on social media @amylabellewinemaker to see what she's cooking for her family.

About LaBelle Winery

LaBelle Winery is New England's premier vineyard and state-of-the-art wine production facility. Founder, winemaker, and entrepreneur Amy LaBelle and her husband and co-owner, Cesar Arboleda, craft more than thirty varieties of award-winning wine. LaBelle Winery's flagship location in Amherst, New Hampshire, offers wine tastings, vineyard and wine cellar tours, bistro dining, two gorgeous event venues, and a retail wine and gift shop.

LaBelle Winery's Derry, New Hampshire, location opened in May 2021 and features two event venues, a golf course, mini-golf, a French-style market and retail shop, a sparkling wine production facility and tasting room, and an award-winning restaurant, Americus. LaBelle Winery Derry is also home to LaBelle Lights, a holiday walking light show featuring more than 500,000 lights and light features.

Award-winning LaBelle Winery makes about 16,000 cases of wine annually and is still growing. They pride themselves on transforming excellent quality fruit into natural, fresh, crisp, fine wine that transforms but maintains its original characters. LaBelle's innovative wines include traditional red and white grape wines and palate-pleasing blends of fruits such as apple, cranberry, raspberry, and blueberry.

LaBelle focuses on making natural, no-chemical-added wine and has received more than 150 medals in national and international wine competitions.

LaBelle Winery is also the launch pad for The Winemaker's Kitchen, a wine-focused culinary product line featuring jams, spice blends, flavored salts, brine and other spice blends, and three savory culinary wines. LaBelle Winery's 20,000 square-foot, state-of-the-art winery and event center is open seven days a week. Wine lovers can taste wine in the grand Tasting Room or relax with cocktails or wine in The Bistro at LaBelle Winery. They can enjoy their choices in the Tasting Room or outside on the terrace, warmed by the fire bowl and overlooking The Vineyards at LaBelle Winery. LaBelle presents at in-store tastings in partnership with retail partners and at many charitable events.

LaBelle Wine can be purchased online at labellewinery.com, at New Hampshire Liquor & Wine Outlets, Shaw's, Market Basket, Hannaford, and many of New Hampshire specialty stores, cafes, and markets. LaBelle Winery also hosts more than 700 events a year, including wedding receptions, social and corporate events.

www.ingramcontent.com/pod-product-compliance
Lightning Source LLC
Chambersburg PA
CBHW060654060526
44119CB00076B/244